Diana Athill was born in 1917. S~~~~~~~~~~~ throughout the Second World War a~~~~~~~~~~~e Deutsch establish the publishing company t~~~~~~~name. Athill's distinguished career as an editor is the subj~~~or her acclaimed memoir *Stet*, which is also published by Granta Books, as are four other volumes of memoirs – *Instead of a Letter*, *After a Funeral*, *Yesterday Morning*, *Make Believe* – and a novel, *Don't Look at Me Like That*.

'Tolstoy was wrong. All happy families are not alike; certainly all happy people are not alike. There are so few of them it's hard to compare. But one thing is clear: Diana Athill is a happy person, and there's no one remotely like her . . . On sex especially everyone over sixty should read her – and everyone under sixty too' *Literary Review*

'Her eye is unflinching, her prose as clear and graceful as ever; her honesty is inspiring' *Spectator*

'Exhilarating and comforting, so much good sense, candour and liveliness of spirit in such clean, clear prose' Simon Gray

'Informative, honest and lacking in the usual sorrow over old age. A remarkable woman' Beryl Bainbridge

'Brave, amusing and graceful' *Sunday Telegraph*

'A convivial memoirist, full of clarity and wit, original thought and understated insight' *Metro*

'[An] honest, clear-sighted book' *Independent*

SOMEWHERE
TOWARDS THE END

DIANA ATHILL

GRANTA

Granta Publications, 12 Addison Avenue, London W11 4QR

First published in Great Britain by Granta Books, 2008
This paperback edition published by Granta Books, 2009

A CIP catalogue record for this book
is available from the British Library.

5 7 9 10 8 6

ISBN 978-1-84708-069-1

Typeset in Minion by M Rules
Printed and bound in Great Britain by
CPI Bookmarque, Croydon

For Sally, Henry, Jessamy and Beauchamp Bagenal

It ain't no sin
To take off your skin
And dance about
In your bones.

Edgar Leslie

1

NEAR THE PARK which my bedroom overlooks there came to stay a family which owned a pack of pugs, five or six of them, active little dogs, none of them overweight as pugs so often are. I saw them recently on their morning walk, and they caused me a pang. I have always wanted a pug and now I can't have one, because buying a puppy when you are too old to take it for walks is unfair. There are dog-walkers, of course; but the best part of owning a dog is walking with it, enjoying its delight when it detects the signs that a walk is imminent, and its glee when its lead is unsnapped and it can bound off over the grass, casting cheerful looks back at you from time to time to make sure that you are still in touch. Our own dog is as old in dog years as I am in human ones (mine amount to eighty-nine), and wants no more than the little potter I can still provide, but I enjoy watching other people's animals busy about their pleasures.

Brought up with dogs, I am baffled by those who dislike them. They have been domesticated for so long that cohabiting with us is as natural to them as the jungle is to the tiger. They have become the only animal whose emotions we can truly penetrate: emotions resembling our own excepting in their simplicity. When a dog is anxious, angry, hungry, puzzled, happy, loving, it allows us to see in their purest form states which we ourselves know, though in us they are distorted by the complex accretions of humanity. Dogs and humans recognize each other at a deep and uncomplicated level. I would so like to begin that process all over again with a little black-velvet-faced pug – but no! It can't be done.

And another thing that can't be done became apparent this morning. I had seen in Thompson & Morgan's plant catalogue a photograph of a tree fern which cost £18, reasonable for something so exotic. A few years ago I fell in love with the tree ferns in the forests of Dominica, and since then I learnt that they, or their cousins, can survive in English gardens, so now I ordered one from that catalogue by phone. It arrived today. Of course I knew that I would not receive a mature tree as shown in the photograph, but I was expecting a sizeable parcel, probably by special delivery. What came, by ordinary post, was a box less than twelve inches long containing a three-inch pot, from which four frail little leaves are sprouting. Whether tree ferns grow quickly or slowly I don't know, but even if it is quickly, it is not possible that I shall ever see this one playing the part I envisaged for it in our garden. I shall pot it on towards that end as far as I can, hoping to see it reach a size at which it can be planted out, but virtuous though planting for the future is supposed to be, it doesn't feel rewarding. It made me think of a turn of phrase often used by Jean Rhys, usually about being drunk: 'I was a bit drunk, well very.' She never in fact said 'I was a bit *sad*, well very' about being old, but no doubt she would have done if she had not hated and feared it too much to speak of it.

Jean was one of my object lessons, demonstrating how not to think about getting old. The prospect filled her with resentment and despair. Sometimes she announced the defiant intention of dyeing her pretty grey hair bright red, but she never did so; less, I think, for the sensible reason that it would have made her look grotesque than because she lacked the energy to organize it. Sometimes – very rarely – drink made her feel better, but more often it turned her querulous and tetchy. She expected old age to make her miserable, and it did, although once she was immersed in it she expressed her misery by complaining about other and lesser things, the big one itself being too much to contemplate – although she did once say that what kept panic at bay was her suicide kit. She had depended on sleeping pills for years and had saved up a substantial cache of them in the drawer of her bedside table, against the day when things got too bad. They did get very bad, but after her death I checked that drawer and the cache was intact.

My second object lesson was the Bulgarian-born, Nobel-Prize-winning writer, Elias Canetti, whose defiance of death was more foolish than Jean's dismay. He had a central European's respect for the construction of abstract systems of thought about the inexplicable, which is uncongenial to many English minds, and which caused him to overvalue his own notions to the extent of publishing two volumes of aphorisms. I never met him, but I knew those books because André Deutsch Limited, the firm in which I worked, published them. During the long years he spent here as a refugee from Nazi Germany, Canetti had taken so violently against the British, I think because they had failed to recognize his genius (the Nobel Prize was yet to come), that he determined never to be published in this country. However Tom Rosenthal, who took over our firm towards the end of its days, had once done him a kindness which he remembered, so he finally agreed to let us have his books on condition that we began with the two lots of aphorisms and followed the American editions, which he had approved, to the last comma, including the jacket copy. This left his English editor (me) nothing to do except read the books, but that was enough to get my hackles up. Many of the aphorisms were pithy and a few were witty, but as a whole what pompous self-importance! The last straw was when his thinking turned to nonsense and he declared, as he did in several of these snippets, that he 'rejected death'.

Later I came to know a former lover of his, the Austrian painter Marie-Louise Motesiczky, a woman who sailed into her eighties gracefully in spite of much physical pain as a result of a severe case of shingles, and a life-story that might well have flattened her. She deserves more than passing attention.

I met her by chance. Mary Hernton, a friend who was looking for a bedsitter in Hampstead, told me she had found a wonderful room in the house of an extraordinary old woman. The room, though wonderful, was not right for her purposes, but the woman had impressed Mary so much that she had invited her to tea and wanted me to meet her. What was so remarkable about her? I would see when I met her, and anyway Mary thought she had been

Canetti's mistress: her shelves were full of books owned by him and the room had once been his. I did join them for tea, and I too was impressed by Marie-Louise. She was funny, warm, charming and indiscreet. When she learnt that I published Canetti she became excited, disregarding the fact that I had never met him, and plunged at once into telling me how they had been friends and lovers for over twenty years before she learnt that he had a wife and daughter. She knew it sounded improbable, but she had lived a secluded life looking after her mother, who had come with her to England from Vienna just before Hitler invaded Austria (they were members of a rich and distinguished Jewish family). Her seclusion seemed to have spared her the knowledge of Canetti's many other women: she never said anything to me suggesting that she knew about them, only that the revelation of his being married had brought their affair to a sudden and agonizing end. The more she told me, the more it seemed to me that Canetti and her mother, who had died quite recently at a great age, had consumed her life and had left her in emptiness . . . except that there was no real feeling of emptiness about Marie-Louise.

Mary had told me that she thought Marie-Louise painted, but when quite soon I visited her in her large Hampstead house, which was full of interesting objects and paintings, I could see nothing that looked as though it had been done by her. She did, however, make a passing reference to her work, so I asked if I might see some of it. I asked nervously – very nervously – because nothing is more embarrassing than being shown paintings that turn out to be dreadful. She led me – and this boded ill – into her bedroom, a large, high-ceilinged room, one whole wall of which was an enormous built-in cupboard. This she opened, to reveal racks crammed with paintings, two of which she pulled out. And I was stunned.

This sweet, funny, frail old woman was indeed a painter, the real thing, up there with Max Beckmann and Kokoschka. It was difficult to know how to take it, because one couldn't say 'Oh my god, you really are a painter!', while if one took her for granted as what she was, one would feel impertinent commenting on her work. I can't remember what I did say, but I must have scrambled through it all right because thereafter she was always happy to talk about her work, for which I was grateful. She was wonderful to talk with about painting, and it explained why there was no feeling of emptiness about her. She was an object lesson on the essential luck, whatever hardships may come their way, of those born able to make things.

There was, however, something to worry about, because what were all those paintings doing, languishing in a bedroom cupboard? It turned out that there were two or three in European public collections and that there had been a show of her work at the Goethe Institute not long ago, but still it was a ridiculous situation for which one couldn't help concluding that Canetti and her mother had been largely responsible. Both were cannibals, Canetti because of self-importance, her mother because of dependence. (Once, she told me, when she said to her mother that she was going out for twenty minutes to buy some necessity, her mother wailed 'But what shall I do if I die before you get back?') Though the fact that during the years of her life in England, German expressionist

8

painting, to which her work was related, had been held in little esteem, may also have contributed to her abdication from the art scene.

But worry was wasted. Although she had been taken advantage of by her two loves, Marie-Louise was a skilful manipulator of everyone else. No sooner did she meet anyone than she began diffidently asking them for help. Could you tell her a good dentist, or plumber, or dressmaker? Might she ask you to help her with this tax return? Always in a way suggesting that you were her only hope. It was quite a while before it dawned on me that a considerable part of the population of Hampstead was waiting on her hand and foot, so that worry wasn't really necessary, and by the time I met her a young friend of hers called Peter Black was well on the way to convincing a great Viennese gallery, the Belvedere, that it must give her the major exhibition that she deserved. I was able to help her write tactful letters to them when she disliked the catalogue descriptions they were providing, which earned me an invitation to the opening. (I also, which pleased me even more, persuaded our National Portrait Gallery to reverse its rejection of her portrait of Canetti. They had told her coldly that they were not interested in portraits of unknown people, and – although I ought not to say it – the letter in which I told them who Canetti was without showing that I knew they didn't know, was a masterpiece. I wish I had kept a copy. The portrait is now there.)

The exhibition in Vienna was a wonderful occasion. Seeing those paintings hung where they ought to be was like seeing animals which had been confined in cages at a zoo released into their natural habitat. I am sure Marie-Louise did not wish to be pleased with anything that her native city did for her (it had murdered her beloved brother, who had stayed behind to help his fellow Jews), but although she made a game attempt at dissatisfaction with details, she could not conceal her pleasure at the whole.

At one of our last meetings before her death I asked her if Canetti had meant it literally when he declared that he would not accept it. Oh yes, she said. And she confessed that there was a time when she was so enthralled by the power of his personality that she had allowed herself to think 'Perhaps he will really do it – will become the first human being not to die.' She was laughing at herself when she said this, but a little tremulously. I think she still felt that his attitude was heroic.

To me it was plain silly. It is so obvious that life works in terms of species rather than of individuals. The individual just has to be born, to develop to the point at which it can procreate, and then to fall away into death to make way for its successors, and humans are no exception whatever they may fancy. We have, however, contrived to extend our falling away so much that it is often longer than our development, so what goes on in it and how to manage it is worth considering. Book after book has been written about being young, and even more of them about the elaborate and testing experiences that cluster round procreation, but there is not much on record about falling away. Being well advanced in that process, and just having had my nose rubbed in it by pugs and tree ferns, I say to myself, 'Why not have a go at it?' So I shall.

2

ALL THROUGH MY sixties I felt I was still within hailing distance of middle age, not safe on its shores, perhaps, but navigating its coastal waters. My seventieth birthday failed to change this because I managed scarcely to notice it, but my seventy-first did change it. Being 'over seventy' is being old: suddenly I was aground on that fact and saw that the time had come to size it up.

I have lived long enough to have witnessed great changes in being old as far as women are concerned – smaller ones for men, but for them less was needed. In my grandmothers' day a woman over seventy adopted what almost amounted to a uniform. If she was a widow she wore black or grey clothes that disregarded fashion, and even if she still had a husband her garments went a bit drab and shapeless, making it clear that this person no longer attempted to be attractive. My paternal grandmother, who was the older of the two, wore floor-length black garments to her dying day, and a little confection of black velvet and lace on her head, a 'cap' such as full-blown Victorian ladies wore. (Judging by the skimpiness of my own hair in old age, which comes from her side of the family, she had good reason for adhering to that particular fashion.) Even one of my aunts, my mother's eldest sister, never wore anything but black or grey after her husband's death in the 1930s, and deliberately chose unsmart shapes for her garments. The abrupt shortening of skirts in the 1920s contributed to the preservation of this 'uniform', because no one at any age wants to look grotesque, and grotesque is what old legs and bodies would have looked in 'flapper' fashions, so in my youth old women were still announcing by their appearance that they had become a different kind of person. After the Second World War, however, reaction against the austerity it had imposed led to far greater flexibility. For a while *Vogue* ran a feature called 'Mrs Exeter' to persuade elderly women that they could wear stylish clothes, and this demonstration soon became unnecessary, so pleased were women to choose clothes to suit their shapes and complexions rather than to conform to a convention. Nowadays an old woman would obviously be daft if she dressed like a teenager, but I have a freedom of choice undreamt of by my grandmothers. There have been days when I went shopping in my local Morrisons wearing something a bit eccentric and wondered whether I would see any raised eyebrows, only to conclude that I would probably have to wear a bikini before anyone so much as blinked.

Even more than clothes, cosmetics have made age look, and therefore feel, less old. Until quite recently they could be a danger, because women who had always worn a lot of make-up tended to continue to do so, blind to the unfortunate effect it could have on an inelastic and crêpy skin. One of my dearest old friends could never get it into her head that if, when doing herself up for a party, she slapped on a lot of scarlet lipstick, it would soon come off on her teeth and begin to run into the little wrinkles round the edge of her lips, making her look like a vampire bat disturbed in mid-dinner. Luckily today's cosmetics are much better made and more subtle in effect, so that an ancient face that would look absurd if *visibly* painted can be gently coaxed into looking quite naturally better than it really is. Having inherited a good skin from my mother, I still receive compliments for it, but nowadays I know that at least half its 'goodness' is thanks to Max Factor. Appearance is important to old women, not because we suppose that it will impress other people, but because of what we ourselves see when we look in a mirror. It is unlikely that anyone else will notice that the nose on an old face is red and shiny or the broken veins on its cheeks are visible, but its owner certainly will, and will equally certainly feel a lift in her spirits when this depressing sight is remedied. And even if how one sees oneself is not wholly how one is, it does contribute a great deal towards it. I know for sure that I both feel and behave younger than my grandmothers did when they were old.

In spite of this, however, the most obvious thing about moving into my seventies was the disappearance of what used to be the most important thing in life: I might not look, or even feel, all that old, but I had ceased to be a sexual being, a condition which had gone through several stages and had not always been a happy one, but which had always seemed central to my existence.

It had started when I was four or five in a way which no doubt appeared comic to onlookers but which felt serious enough to me, with the announcement that I was going to marry John Sherbroke. He was a little boy who lived a few houses up from us on the street beside Woolwich Common (my father, an officer in the Royal Artillery, was presumably an instructor at the Military Academy there at the time, and John's father was also a Gunner). I can't remember John at all, except for his name, and that he was my Intended. His successor is clearer in my memory because of his beautiful, sad brown eyes and the glamour bestowed on him by his great age – he was Denis, the gardener's boy at the Hall Farm where we had gone to live under the wing of my mother's parents. I doubt whether I ever spoke to Denis, but I did, with great daring, spit on his head out of the lavatory window when he was working the pump by the back door. He was followed by loves with whom I did communicate – indeed I and my brother spent much time with them: Jack and Wilfred, sons of the head cow-man at the farm, remembered even more clearly than Denis because of the amount of time I put into trying to decide which I loved best.

Those two were the first beneficiaries of my romantic phase, in which love took the form of daydreams. The object of my passion would be placed in a situation of great danger – his house on fire, perhaps, or he was being swept away in a flood – and I would rescue him, the dream's climax being that when he recovered consciousness he would open his eyes to find me leaning over him, my cloud of black hair enveloping him like a cloak (I was a skinny child with a mouse-coloured bob, but I confidently expected to improve with time). Jack and Wilfred lasted until I was nine, when they were ousted by the first love I chose for real reasons: David, who was far kinder, braver and more sensible than the rest of us and was also a familiar friend and companion. He, too, was liable to be rescued, though rather guiltily because of how silly he would have thought it, had he known. He told his mother I was a good sport, which was thrilling at the time, though as I entered my teens it did begin to pall.

Then, at fifteen, I fell in love as an adult. It was with Paul (I called him that in *Instead of a Letter*, so he can keep the name here), who came during one of his Oxford vacations to earn a bit of money by coaching my brother for an exam. He dispelled daydreams by being the real thing, but he did not dispel romance. I loved, I assumed love equalled marriage, and I was certain that once I was married to the man I loved I would be faithful to him for the rest of my life. I did have the occasional, fleeting daydream about my beautiful white wedding, but to embroider my romanticism beyond that, once I was old enough to hold Paul's attention and we became engaged, was not easy, partly because of how everyone went on at me about how poor we would be and how I would have to learn to be a good housewife. Paul, who had gone into the RAF, was still only a pilot-officer whose pay was £400 a year, which seemed to him and me enough to have a good time on, whatever 'they' said, but still the warnings were sobering; though less so than something which happened about six months after we announced our engagement.

We went, with his sister, to a party with a group of rather louche friends of Paul's – I didn't know where he had picked them up, and was disconcerted by them from the start because they were drinking harder and talking more crudely than anyone I had met hitherto. One of them had brought along an extravagantly sexy-looking girl who made a dead set at Paul the moment she saw him, and to my incredulous dismay he responded. After an extremely uncomfortable hour or two he shovelled the task of seeing me home onto his embarrassed sister, and he ended the evening, I was sure, in bed with that girl. During the following two weeks I heard nothing from him, and felt too crushed to write or call myself, and when he let me know that he was about to fly down from Grantham to spend the weekend at Oxford with me, as he often did, I was more anxious than relieved.

During the Saturday evening we drank too much and he collapsed into almost tearful apology. He had behaved horribly, he was so ashamed of himself he couldn't bear it, I must, must believe that it had meant absolutely nothing, that girl had turned out to be a ghastly bore (what a slip-up! Suppose she hadn't been?). Never again would he do anything like that because I was and always would be the only woman he really loved, and so on and so on. It was better than silence had been, but it was not good.

Next morning we took a taxi to 'our' pub in Appleton and dismissed it before we got there in order to dispel our headaches by walking the last mile, although it was a bitterly cold and windy winter day. Paul seemed relaxed, scanning the fields on either side of the muddy lane for fieldfares; I was dismally silent, mulling over his apology. It had meant nothing: yes, I accepted that. But his declaration that such a thing would never happen again: no, that I was unable to believe. I don't remember being as shocked as I ought to have been at his doing it under my nose, thus betraying a really gross indifference to my feelings. I had a humble opinion of my own importance, carefully fostered by a family which considered vanity a serious sin, so in such a situation I tended to blame myself as not being worthy of consideration, and I wasn't consciously thinking of that although I am now sure that it was gnawing away at me. What I knew I was thinking about was how this flightiness of Paul's must be handled. I remember thinking that once we were married I would have to learn to be *really clever*. 'It will be all right for quite a time,' I thought. 'He will go on coming back to me while we are like we are now. But when I get old – when I'm *thirty* – and I saw a flash of my own face, anxious and wrinkled under grey hair – 'then it will be dangerous, then he could fall in love with one of them.' Would I learn to be clever *enough*? I'd have to. The whole of that day remained dismal, but not for a moment did it occur to me that I might not want to marry him, and soon our relationship was restored to its usual enjoyable state.

So I don't think there was ever a time in my adult life when I didn't realize that men were quite likely to be technically unfaithful to women, although it was not until Paul had finally jilted me that I saw that women, too, could be cheered up by sex without love. I 'recovered' from Paul in that I fell in love again, twice, and heavily, but both times it felt 'fatal', something impossible to avoid, and anyway I longed for it, but which was bound to bring pain. The first time it was with a married man much older than myself, and I never envisaged him leaving his wife for me. No doubt if he had suggested it I would have accepted, but I admired him far too much to expect it: I was his wartime fling, or folly (there's nothing like a whiff of death in the air to intensify desire, the essence of life – I remember him whispering in amazement 'I'd resigned myself to never feeling like this again'), while she was his good and blameless wife who had just become the mother of their first child, so leaving her would prove him cruel and irresponsible which I was sure he was not. I would not have loved him so much if he had been.

My second after-Paul love was available, even eligible, but his very eligibility seemed to make him too good to be true. He liked me a lot. For a time he almost thought he was in love with me, but he never quite was and I sensed almost from the beginning that it was going to end in tears, whereupon I plunged in deeper and deeper. And it did end in tears quite literally, both of us weeping as we walked up and down Wigmore Street on our last evening together. With masochistic abandon I loved him even more for his courage in admitting the situation and sparing me vain hopes (and in fact such courage, which takes a lot of summoning up, is something to be grateful for, because a broken heart mends much faster from a conclusive blow than it does from slow strangulation. Believe me! Mine experienced both.)

That, for me, was the end of romantic love. What followed, until I met Barry Reckord in my forty-fourth year, was a series of sometimes very brief, sometimes sustained affairs, always amiable (two of them very much so), almost always cheering-up (two of the tiny ones I could have done without), and none of them going deep enough to hurt. During those years, if a man wanted to marry me, as three of them did, I felt what Groucho Marx felt about a club willing to accept him: disdain. I tried to believe it was something more rational, but it wasn't. Several of the painless affairs involved other people's husbands, but I never felt guilty because the last thing I intended or hoped for was damage to anyone's marriage. If a wife ever found out – and as far as I know that never happened – it would have been from her husband's carelessness, not mine.

Loyalty is not a favourite virtue of mine, perhaps because André Deutsch used so often to abuse the word, angrily accusing any writer who wanted to leave our list of 'disloyalty'. There is, of course, no reason why a writer should be loyal to a firm which has supposed that it will be able to make money by publishing his work. Gratitude and affection can certainly develop when a firm makes a good job of it, but no bond of loyalty is established. In cases where such a bond exists – loyalty to family, for example, or to a political party – it can become foolishness if betrayed by its object. If your brother turns out to be a murderer or your party changes its policies, standing by him or it through thick or thin seems to me mindless. Loyalty unearned is simply the husk of a notion developed to benefit the bosses in a feudal system. When spouses are concerned, it seems to me that kindness and consideration should be the key words, not loyalty, and sexual infidelity does not necessarily wipe them out.

Fidelity in the sense of keeping one's word I respect, but I think it tiresome that it is tied so tightly in people's minds to the idea of sex. The belief that a wife owes absolute fidelity to her husband has deep and tangled roots, being based not only on a man's need to know himself to be the father of his wife's child, but also on the even deeper, darker feeling that man *owns* woman, God having made her for his convenience. It's hard to imagine the extirpation of that: think of its power in Islam! And woman's anxious clamour for her husband's fidelity springs from the same primitive root: she feels it to be necessary proof of her value. That I know only too well, having had the stuffing knocked out of me so painfully when Paul chose to marry someone else. But understanding doesn't mean approving. Why, given our bone-deep, basic need for one another, do men and women have to put so much weight on this particular, unreliable aspect of it?

I think now of Isaac Bashevis Singer's story, 'The Peephole in the Gate', about a young man who saw his sweetheart home on the eve of their marriage, couldn't resist taking one last look at her through the peephole – and there she was, being soundly and obviously enjoyably kissed by the porter. End of betrothal – though the narrator does slyly remind the young man that he had it off with a serving maid that same afternoon. The story goes on to suggest how much simpler, and probably better, two people's lives would have been if that sexual infidelity had never come to light: a theme which Singer, that wise old bird, returns to several times, always with his characteristic trick of leaving the pronouncement of a moral judgement in the hands of the reader. Given his deep attachment to his religious background, I can't be sure that he would have agreed with the judgement I produce – but after all, he *does* ask for it. Yes, there are some things, sexual infidelities among them, that do no harm if they remain unknown – or, for that matter, are known and accepted, and which is preferable depends on the individuals and their circumstances. I only have to ask myself which I would choose, if forced to do so, between the extreme belief that a whole family's honour is stained by an unfaithful wife unless she is killed, and the attitude often attributed to the French, that however far from admirable sexual infidelity is, it is perfectly acceptable if *conducted properly*. Vive la France!

This attitude I shared, and still share, with Barry, with whom, after I had finally shed the scars of a broken heart (by 'writing them out', as I will explain later), I eventually settled down into an extraordinarily happy loving friendship, which remained at its best for about eight years until it began to be affected not by emotional complications, but by Time. This was not a sudden event, but its early stage, which took place during my mid- and late fifties, was followed by a reprieve, which made it possible to ignore its significance. Gradually I had become aware that my interest in, and therefore my physical response to, making love with my dear habitual companion, was dwindling: familiarity had made the touch of his hand feel so like the touch of my own hand that it no longer conveyed a thrill. Looking back, I wonder why I never talked about this with him, because I didn't. I simply started to fake. Probably this was because the thought of 'working at' the problem together, as I supposed a marriage counsellor would suggest, struck me as unlikely to solve it. Tedious and absurd: that was how I envisaged such a procedure. If something that had always worked naturally now didn't work – well, first you hoped that faking it would bring it back, which sometimes it did, and when that stopped happening you accepted that it was over.

That acceptance was sad. Indeed, I was forced into it, at a time when our household was invaded by a ruthless and remarkably succulent blonde in her mid-twenties and he fell into bed with her. There was one sleepless night of real sorrow, but only one night. What I mourned during that painful night was not the loss of my loving old friend who was still there, and still is, but the loss of youth: 'What she has, god rot her, I no longer have and will never, never have again.' A belated recognition, up against which I had come with a horrid crunch. But very soon another voice began to sound in my head, which made more sense. 'Look,' it said, 'you know quite well that you have stopped wanting him in your bed, it's months since you enjoyed it, so what are you moaning about? Of course you have lost youth, you have moved on and stopped wanting what youth wants.' And that was the end of that stage.

Soon afterwards came the reprieve, when I found, to my amusement and pleasure, that novelty could restore sex. I described in *Instead of a Letter* how after an early, real and long-lasting sorrow my morale had begun to be restored by an affair with a man I called Felix, which did not involve love but was thoroughly enjoyable otherwise. Now, as I approached my sixties, it happened again, and my life as a sexual being was prolonged by seven years while Barry went his own way, our companionship having become more like that of brother and sister than of lovers. A second man with whom I had little in common won himself a place in memory made warm by gratitude. After him there was no reprieve, nor did I want one.

THE LAST MAN in my life as a sexual being, who accompanied me over the frontier between late middle-age and being old, was Sam, who was born in Grenada in the Caribbean. Whether he had come to England in order to volunteer for the war, or his arrival just happened to coincide with its outbreak, I don't know. He joined the RAF Regiment, in which he worked as a clerk, and in his own time came to know Padmore and other black elders of that day who were concerned with establishing the black man's rights in Britain. He gained a good deal of experience in broadcasting at this time, which served him well later, when he moved on to Ghana and soon attracted the attention of Kwame Nkrumah, who put him in charge of his government's public relations so that he became in effect a member of it, although he was never a minister. He remained Nkrumah's trusted servant and friend until the coup which brought the Redeemer down, simultaneously putting an end to Sam's palmy days in Africa. Because he was known in Accra as an honest man who took no bribes he escaped prison, but he had to leave the country at four days' notice taking nothing but his clothes. When I met him, all he had left from those palmy days was a beautiful camel-hair overcoat with a sable collar, and the gold watch on a handsome bracelet given him by Haile Selassie.

Being an impressive-looking man, very tall, with pleasant manners, easy-going but sensible, clearly on the side of good sense and decorum, he had no trouble getting a job almost at once in the British Government's organization concerned with race relations. He was just settling into it when we met at a party at which there were several old African hands of one sort and another. My partner at André Deutsch had kick-started a publishing firm in Nigeria during the 1960s and we had some African writers on our list, so the newly independent countries, and race relations, were part of the landscape in which I existed at that time.

In addition to that, in the course of my close and happy relationship with Barry, which had by then lasted about eight years, I had come to feel more at home with black men than with white. Barry, having been educated by English schoolmasters at his Jamaican school and by English dons at Cambridge, used sometimes to say that his fellow Jamaicans saw him as 'a small, square, brown Englishman', and some of them may have done so, but he was black enough to have received his share of insults from white men; and one can't identify with someone of whom that is true without feeling more like him than like his insulters.

The first black person with whom I was ever in the same room was an African undergraduate at a party during my first term at

Oxford in 1936. Dancing was going on, and I was deeply relieved at his not asking me for a dance. I knew that if he asked I would have to say yes, and I hadn't the faintest idea why the prospect seemed so appalling. It was just something which would have appalled my parents, so it appalled me. But I am glad to say that when, a week later, a friend said to me, 'I think I would be sick if a black man touched me,' I was shocked. I don't remember thinking about it in the intervening days, but somehow I had taken the first tiny step of seeing that my reaction to the idea of dancing with that man had been disgusting.

After that I must gradually have given the matter enough thought to get my head straight about it, because when I next came in touch with black people, which didn't happen for some years, I was able to see them as individuals. The first time I was kissed by a black man – a friendly peck at the end of a taxi-ride from one pub to another – I did note it as an occasion, because the fact that it was just like being kissed by anyone else proved me right in a satisfactory way: I was still feeling pleased with myself for not having racist feelings. But by the time I met Barry, although I had never had occasion to make love with a black man I had met many black people and worked with some of them, so clicking with him at a party and soon afterwards going to bed with him didn't seem particularly noteworthy except for being much more fun than the last such encounter I'd had, because this time we liked each other so well. It was only after we had settled into togetherness that I started expecting to like black men better than whites. I always might, of course, end up disliking the one or liking the other contrary to expectation, but I did, from then on, start out with a bias towards the black, or at any rate the un-English.

So when at our first meeting Sam made a stately swoop, I was pleased: it was both funny and revivifying to be seen as attractive by this agreeable and sexy person, just after concluding that my love-making days were over. Soon after that he moved into a flat near Putney Bridge, and for the next seven years I spent a night with him there about once a week.

We rarely did anything together except make ourselves a pleasant little supper and go to bed, because we had very little in common apart from liking sex. Sam had an old-fashioned sense of what was proper, but I am sure it had never entered his head to think of sex in connection with guilt. As well as *The Pickwick Papers*, *The Bab Ballads* and several booklets about the Rosicrucians and the Christian Scientists, *The Kama Sutra* was among the books permanently entangled in his bedclothes. We also shared painful feet, which was almost as important as liking sex, because when you start feeling your age it is comforting to be with someone in the same condition. You recognize it in each other, but there is no need to go on about it. We never mentioned our feet, just kicked our shoes off as soon as we could.

To be more serious, the really important thing we had in common was that neither of us had any wish to fall in love or to become responsible for someone else's peace of mind. We didn't even need to see a great deal of each other. We knew that we would give each other no trouble.

So what did we give each other?

I gave Sam sex that suited him. The first, but not most enduring, attraction was that I was white and well-bred. Sam had nothing against black women (except his wife, whom he saw as a burden imposed on him by his mother before he'd developed the sense to understand what a mistake it was); but since he came to England at the end of the 1930s all his most important women had been white. He had been bettering himself ever since his mother urged him to work hard at school, and claiming a white woman for yourself would, alas, be recognized by most black men from his background, at that time, as part of that process. This was a fact that gave older and/or not particularly glamorous white women an edge with black men that they hadn't got for white ones, which is evidently deplorable although I can't help being grateful for it. Sam was not a man of vulgar instincts so he didn't want to show his woman off, but it gave him private satisfaction to feel that she was worth showing. Then it turned out that physically I was right for him, and that I could be good company. So I was satisfying as a status symbol, agreeable as a companion in so far as he wanted one, and was able and willing to play along with him in a way he enjoyed. He obviously felt he need look no further.

Sam's chief attraction to me was that he wanted me: to be urgently wanted at a time when I no longer expected it cheered me up and brought me alive again – no small gift. Also, I am curious. His background and the whole course of his life, being so different from mine, seemed interesting even when he was being dull. A middle-class Englishman with his nature would have bored me because I would have known too much about him. Sam I wanted to find out about, and what I found out was likeable. Even when I was thinking 'What an old noodle!' I liked him, and what I liked best was the sense I picked up of the boy he used to be.

He had the calm self-confidence and general benevolence bestowed by a secure and happy childhood. A middle-class adoring mother can sometimes damage her child, but in a peasant family she is more likely to make him: she must get him out of this hard life if she possibly can, even if she loses him in the process. Sam's father owned the patch of land on which they lived (and that, too, contributed to self-confidence, because being raised on your own place, however small, is stabilizing), but it was a property too small to support a family so he had to find work in Trinidad, and then in Venezuela. It was the mother who ran the home, and she gave her son unquestioned precedence over her two daughters (Barry's mother did the same thing and her daughter never quite forgave her).

'We didn't know it,' Sam told me, 'but the food we ate was just what everyone says nowadays is the healthiest: fish, fruit and vegetables, we were never short of those.' They lived right on the sea so escaped the common West Indian overdependence on root vegetables. 'And all that air and exercise. I thought nothing of running five miles to school and five miles back – long-distance running was a craze with us boys, we ran everywhere.' They rode, too. Most people kept a horse (this surprised me) and if a boy wanted to get somewhere in a hurry he could jump on to some neighbour's bare-backed nag without having to ask. And they swam as much as they ran. He marvelled when he remembered how no one fussed when they used to swim out to a little islet about two miles offshore. A very tall, good-looking, even-tempered boy, good at all the local pastimes, crammed with healthy food and plunged by his fond mother into herb baths of which she knew the secrets, Sam was evidently secure among his friends as a leader. When he recalled those happy times he seemed to bring glimpses of them into the room – a whiff of nutmeg-scented sea-breeze, very endearing.

His mother lost him, of course – that wife was her big mistake. He begot two children on her, then could stand it no longer, left for England and his mother never saw him again. She died asking for him, people wrote and told him that. He spoke of it solemnly but placidly: it was a mother's fate, he implied, sad but inevitable.

He did not consider himself a bad son, husband or father for having left. He had kept in touch, sent money, seen to it that his children were educated: he had done what was proper. His son became a doctor and moved to the United States, and they saw each other from time to time. His daughter was unforgiving, 'a stupid girl'. And his wife . . . Thirty-five years after he left Grenada he returned for the first time, for a three-week visit at the invitation of the prime minister. He didn't let his wife know he was coming, but after the first week it occurred to him to drop in on her, still without warning. 'So what happened?' I asked. He shook his head, clicked his tongue, and said slowly and disapprovingly: 'That's a very *cantankerous* woman'. This made me laugh so much that he took offence and provided no more details. Not that he would have been able to provide any of real interest, since he obviously had no conception of the life to which he had condemned that 'stupid' daughter and that 'cantankerous' wife: a convenient ignorance shared by a great number of West Indian husbands and 'baby-fathers' – though many of the women left behind seem to take it calmly.

Our relationship ended gently, the gaps between our meetings becoming gradually longer. The last time we met, after an especially long one (so long that, without regret, I had thought it final), he was slower than usual and seemed abstracted and tired, but not ill. Although we had agreed already that our affair was over, he said 'What about coming to bed?' but I could see he was relieved when I said no. 'The trouble with me,' I said, 'is that the spirit is willing but the flesh is weak. My body has gone against it.' He didn't say 'Mine too', he wouldn't want to go as far as that, but he did say: 'I know, the body does go against things. You can't do anything about that.' And the next thing I heard about him, not very much later, was that he had died suddenly of a heart attack.

You can't miss someone grievously if you haven't seen them or wanted to see them for several months and they had touched only a comparatively small corner of your life, but after his death Sam became more vivid in my mind than many of my more important dead. I saw him with photographic clarity – still can. His gestures, his expressions, the way he walked and sat, his clothes. The seven years of him played through my head with the immediacy of a newsreel: all we said, all we did, perhaps the pattern of our meetings was so repetitive that I couldn't help learning him by heart. I particularly remember the feel of him. His skin was smooth and always seemed to be cool and dry, a pleasant, healthy skin, and his smell was pleasant and healthy. I feel him lying beside me after making love, both of us on our backs, hands linked, arms and legs touching in a friendly way. His physical presence is so clear, even now, that it is almost like a haunt (an amiable one).

The faith Sam had decided to favour was in the transmigration of souls because, he said, how else could one explain why one person had a good life and another a horrid one: they were getting what they had earned in their previous lives, it was obvious. He was displeased when I said that if that were so, how odd that so many black people must have been very wicked in the past. He refused to take it up because, I think, transmigration was promising to him personally. He had, after all, been uncommonly lucky: a little refinement of the soul towards the end and up he would go. That, he once explained to me, was why he had given up meat and hard liquor once he was past sixty. I wish I could hope that Sam was right in expecting to come back to earth for another life. If he could, I doubt whether it would be so rarefied a life as he had aimed for, but it would certainly be several degrees more enjoyable than the one he left, which would make it much better than most. Meanwhile, perhaps because he carried into the beginning of my old age something belonging to younger days, he is still alive in my head, and I am glad of it. Dear Sam.

A N IMPORTANT ASPECT of the ebbing of sex was that other things became more interesting. Sex obliterates the individuality of young women more often than it does that of young men, because so much more of a woman than of a man is used by sex. I have tried to believe that most of this difference comes from conditioning, but can't do so. Conditioning reinforces it, but essentially it is a matter of biological function. There is no physical reason why a man shouldn't turn and walk away from any act of sex he performs, whereas every act of sex performed by a woman has the potential of changing her mode of being for the rest of her life. He simply triggers the existence of another human being; she has to build it out of her own physical substance, carry it inside her, bond with it whether she likes it or not – and to say that she has been freed from this by the pill is nonsense. She can prevent it, but only by drastic chemical intervention which throws her body's natural behaviour out of gear. Having bodies designed to bear children means that many generations will have to pass before women are

e psychic patterns dictated by their physique, however
ᴇᴀꜱ   them to swallow a pill; and it is possible that they will
never be able to achieve such psychic freedom. Exactly how much
of personality is determined by chemistry is at present beyond
assessment, but that some of it is can't be doubted. Because of all
this, when they are at the peak of their physical activity women
often disappear into it, many of them discovering what kind of
people they are apart from it only in middle age, some of them
never. I had started to have glimpses of myself earlier than most, as
a result of being deprived of marriage and child-bearing, but not
with the clarity I discovered once sex had fallen right away. My
atheism is an example: it became much more firmly established.

I had known for a long time that I did not believe in a god, an
attitude which had crystallized when I was at Oxford towards the
end of the 1930s and met a man called Duncan at a party. We were
not to become friends because it was the end of term, and the term
was Duncan's last. He had finished his final exams that day, had
already been accepted by the Colonial Service, and would be taking
up a post in Cyprus in a few weeks' time. We were drawn to each
other, however, left the party together, had dinner and went punt-
ing on the river, and the next day we met again and spent the
afternoon in his rooms. At that time I was stuck in the unhappiness
of betrayed love, feeling shrivelled because it was months since I
had heard from Paul. Being in the habit of considering myself
unavailable to other men, I told Duncan I was engaged, but I am
sure that if we had gone on seeing each other I would have been
rescued: he was the most agreeable and intelligent man I had met

at Oxford, and the morning after our afternoon together he sent me flowers with a note saying, 'We will see each other again'. We never did. I had two letters from him, the second from Cyprus, and then the war began and I forgot him. Except that I kept, and still keep, one thing he said.

We must have talked at supper about what we believed, because after it, as we walked over grass through the sweet summer night to the place where the punts were moored, I said that though I was unable to believe in the god I had been taught to believe in, I supposed that some kind of First Cause had to be accepted. To which Duncan replied 'Why? Might it not be that beginnings and endings are things we think in terms of simply because our minds are too primitive to conceive of anything else?'

Did I answer? I can remember only tilting my head back and gazing up into the star-filled sky with a feeling of extreme, almost dizzy elation, as though for the first time my eyes were capable of seeing space as it deserved to be seen. I made no attempt to plumb the implications of this idea, but neither did I hesitate to accept it as the truth. And for a long time that was the extent of my thinking about religion.

I was brought back to it when I was beginning to be old by John Updike, when he was analysing (I don't remember where) his own religious belief, and said, or rather wrote: 'Among the repulsions of atheism for me has been its drastic uninterestingness as an intellectual position. Where was the ambiguity, the ingenuity, the humanity (in the Harvard sense) of saying that the universe just happened to happen and that when we're dead we're dead?' This baffled me. Perhaps it is uninteresting intellectually to believe that the nature of the universe is far, far beyond grasping, not only by oneself as an individual but by oneself as a member of our species; but emotionally, or poetically, it seems to me vastly more exciting and more beautiful than exercising any amount of ingenuity in making up fairy stories.

John Updike would agree that our planet is a mere speck in that small part of the universe which we are capable of perceiving, and that *Homo sapiens* has existed for only a tiny fraction of that planet's tiny time, and has not the slightest idea of what 90 per cent of the universe is made of (I like scientists calling what they don't know 'dark matter'); so how can he, or any other intelligent person, fail to agree that men are being absurdly kind to themselves when they suppose that something thought by them is universally relevant (those religious people who believe in one god do seem to see him as universal, not as local to Earth)? Faith – the decision to act as though you believe something you have no reason to believe, hoping that the decision will bring on belief and then you will feel better – that seems to me mumbo-jumbo. I can't feel anything but sure that when men form ideas about God, creation, eternity, they are making no more sense in relation to what lies beyond the range of their comprehension than the cheeping of sparrows. And given that the universe continues to be what it is, regardless of what we believe, and what it is has always been and will continue to be the condition of our existence, why should the thought of our smallness in it be boring – or, for that matter, frightening?

I have heard people bewailing man's landing on the moon, as

though before it was touched by an astronaut's foot it was made of silver or mother-of-pearl, and that footprint turned it into grey dust. But the moon never was made of silver or mother-of-pearl, and it still shines as though it were so made. Whether we know less or more about it, it remains itself and continues to reflect the sun's light in a way that is beautiful in men's eyes. Surely the part of life which is within our range, the mere fact of life, is mysterious and exciting enough in itself? And surely the urgent practical necessity of trying to order it so that its cruelties are minimized and its beauties are allowed their fullest possibly play is compelling enough without being seen as a duty laid on us by a god?

People of faith so often seem to forget that a god who gives their lives meaning too often provides them with justification when they want to wipe out other people who believe in other gods, or in nothing. My own belief – that we on our short-lived planet are part of a universe simultaneously perfectly ordinary in that *there it is* and incalculably mysterious in that it is beyond our comprehension – does not feel like believing in nothing and would never make me recruit anyone for slaughter. It feels like a state of infinite possibility, stimulating and enjoyable – not exactly comforting, but acceptable because true. And this remains so when I force myself to think about the most alarming aspect of what I can understand, which is that we will eventually become extinct, differing from the dinosaurs only in contributing a good deal more than they did to our own fate. And it also remains so when I contemplate my personal extinction.

I once had a favourite image for falling asleep which I used when getting into bed felt particularly good. After waiting a minute or two before switching off my lamp, collecting awareness so that I would fully appreciate the embrace of darkness, I turned face downwards, sprawled my arms and legs, and my bed became a raft which floated me out onto the sea of night. It produced a sensation of luxury, the more seductive for being enlivened by an almost imperceptible thread of risk.

Once we at André Deutsch brought out a coffee-table book about beds prefaced by an oddly inappropriate essay by Anthony Burgess. The book was supposed to be in praise of beds, but Burgess said he loathed them because he was afraid of going to sleep and needed to outwit his fear by letting sleep catch him unexpectedly in a chair or on the floor. Lying down on a bed, he felt, was like lying down on a bier from which, if he lost consciousness, he might never get up. (I did question this preface, but André's view was that no one bothered to read prefaces, what mattered was having the man's name on the book, not what he said – a bit of publisher-think which I deplored, but not strongly enough to make a stand.) I have read of people undergoing many things worse than this quirk of Burgess's, but of no ordeal that was harder for me to imagine sharing. Being forced to deny oneself one of the greatest pleasures of everyday life, the natural seal of happiness, the sure escape from sorrow or boredom, the domestication of mystery . . . What an affliction! Could the poor man really have been so savagely haunted by the fear of death? From which it may correctly be deduced that I myself have never been enough troubled by it to want to envisage an afterlife.

What explains irreligiosity? Lack of imagination? Courage? A genetically bestowed pattern of temperament? The first two occur in the religious as well as the irreligious, and the third only shunts the question back through the generations. Religious people of limited intelligence often think that the explanation is licentiousness, a naughty refusal to accept restraints; but many an unbeliever is as scrupulous as any religious person in acknowledging the restrictions and obligations laid on us by sharing the world with others. To the irreligious person the answer seems simple enough, though embarrassing to pronounce: he is more intelligent than his religious brother. But his religious brother sees with equal clarity that the opposite is true, and where is the neutral referee? We must settle, I suppose, for there being in this respect two kinds of person.

My kind enjoys an unfair advantage. In the Western world there are probably nowadays as many people without the religious instinct as with it, but all of them live in societies which developed on lines laid down by believers: everywhere on earth men started by conjuring Powers into being to whom they could turn for direction and control of their behaviour. The mechanism was obviously a necessary one in its time. So we, the irreligious, live within social structures built by the religious, and however critical or resentful we may be of parts of them, no honest atheist would deny that in so far as the saner aspects of religion hold within a society, that society is the better for it. We take a good nibble of our brother's cake before throwing it away.

Right behaviour, to me, is the behaviour taught me by my Christian family: one should do unto one's neighbour as one would like him to do unto one, should turn the other cheek, should not pass on the other side of those in trouble, should be gentle to children, should avoid obsession with material possessions. I have accepted a great deal of Christ's teaching partly because it was given me in childhood by people I loved, and partly because it continues to make sense and the nearer people come to observing it the better I like them (not that they come, or ever have come, very near it, and nor have I). So my piece of my brother's cake is a substantial chunk, and it is covered, what's more, with a layer of icing, because much of the painting and sculpture I love best (and such things matter a lot to me) was made by artists who lived long enough ago to believe that heaven and hell were real. In the Correr Museum in Venice, coming suddenly on Dieric Bouts's little *Madonna nursing the Child*, I was struck through with delight as I never was by a mother and child by, for example, Picasso or Mary Casson, and I cannot remember being more intensely moved by any painting than by Piero della Francesca's *Nativity*.

It is not the artist's skill that works the spell, charming though it is in Bouts's case and awe-inspiring in della Francesca's. It is the selflessness of such art that is magnetic, as it is in a Chinese bronze of the Buddha, a medieval wood-carving of an angel, or an African mask. The person making the object wasn't trying to express his own personality or his own interpretation of appearances; he was trying to represent something outside himself for which he felt the utmost respect, love or dread – to show us this wonderful thing as well as he possibly could. How the purity of this intention makes itself felt in the artefact I don't understand, but it does. You need only compare any halfway respectable Madonna and child from the fourteenth or fifteenth century with even the best modern one to see that it does, and that it is something to do with the artist's taking for granted the truth of what he is representing. From the seventeenth century on there is always a taint of sentimentality or hysteria in religious art, however splendid the technique, and by the twentieth century it soaks the object right through: think of the junkety smugness of Eric Gill! Of course great artists painting non-religious works often attend to what they are making with a respect and love which takes them beyond self and approaches the same purity, but there is no longer a subject strong enough to save the bacon of an artist less than great (Bouts was good, not great).

Early religious music, lovely though much of it is, has a less powerful effect on me: I prefer Bach's instrumental music to his cantatas. The words, I suppose, make the cantatas too dogmatic for me: even the greatest religious poetry and prose leaves me unmoved. The painter of a triptych for an altar did it with dog-matic intent, but his medium is less suited to teaching than words are. Dogmatically, painting is a blunt instrument, so the lily, the goldfinch, the pomegranate, the dove, the mother, the child can all be taken to exist for their own sakes, regardless of their message. Although – baffling paradox – it is precisely their creator's belief in the truth of the message that gives them their force.

My indifference to religious writing is overcome by one majestic exception: the Bible. I was brought up to know both the Old Testament and the New fairly well, and am still glad of it. The beauty of the language has much to do with this, but my maternal grandmother's gift for reading aloud to children has much more. She left us in no doubt that we were listening to very *special* true stories – special because their truth concerned us closely. Nowadays, if I read the story of Joseph and his brethren, or of Shadrach, Meshach and Abednego, or of the nativity, or of the raising of Lazarus, something odd but enjoyable happens. This laptop offers the choice of a number of different typefaces and I can tell it which to use with a touch of a finger. When I read those stories it is as though at a finger-touch my adult mind is replaced by my child mind. There go the familiar stories, unfolding before my eyes, sounding and looking just as they sounded and looked when Gran read them to me. Of course I can still think about them in an adult way and of course it does not mean that I kneel down and worship God: I love the story of how he called Samuel in the night, but he still doesn't call me. It is simply that those stories are engraved in my imagination so deeply that they can't be erased by disbelief. They have, in fact, nothing to do with belief or disbelief as I mean the words now, but they restore the sensation of belief as it used to be in the same way that Christmas carols do. They still trail a whiff of that old special importance, to be caught by some part of my awareness which is usually dormant. The Bible was shown to me through the prism of belief, the absolute belief of those who wrote it and the diluted but still real belief of my grandmother, who did not think God was like the Jehovah of the Jews but still believed that he existed, and who probably saw Jesus's son-ship, immaculate conception and so on as metaphor but still held that in order to be good people we must believe in his divinity. Coming to me in this persuasive way it did certainly influence the way I was to see life; yet it failed to convince me of its central teaching. How, then, does the written word work? What part of a reader absorbs it – or should that be a double question: what part of a reader absorbs what part of a text?

I think that underneath, or alongside, a reader's conscious response to a text, whatever is needy in him is taking in whatever the text offers to assuage that need.

For example, I have a much younger friend, Sally, who when her children were just beginning to read became annoyed because so many of the books written for them were about animals: it was a mouse, not a child, which disobeyed its mother and got into trouble, a rabbit who raided the kitchen garden, an elephant who became king. Why, she asked, was she expected to feed her children on this pap of fantasy instead of on stories about real life? The answer, it seems to me, is that children respond to animal protagonists because when very small what they need is not to discover and recognize 'real life', but to discover and recognize their own feelings. Take a pair of well-known animal characters, Piglet and Tigger, in *The House at Pooh Corner*. Piglet is an anxious, timid little person, capable of being brave if he absolutely has to be, but only at great cost to himself, and Tigger is so exuberantly bouncy that he can be a nuisance. Both of them express things which a child discovers and recognizes with pleasure because they exist within himself. If those characteristics were expressed on the page by a child, they would belong to that child and would call for the use of

49

the kind of critical faculty one employs vis-à-vis another person. Expressed by a 'made up' animal (I have yet to meet a child so simple-minded that it doesn't know perfectly well that animals don't talk in human language), they slip past the critical faculty into the undergrowth of feelings which need so urgently to be sorted out and understood. (When a story about people, not animals, is *popular* with the very young – the Postman Pat stories, for example – the people are drawn in such an unrealistic way that they might as well be animals.) What was important for Sally's little children was not to be given only sensible, real-life stories, but to have plenty of them about for when they began to need them.

When I was in my early teens I used to sink luxuriously into a romantic novel as though into a hot bath, and couldn't have too many of them. I never believed, however, that anyone in real life looked or behaved like the heroes and heroines of those books. What I needed was to practise the sensations of sex – to indulge in a kind of non-genital masturbation – because I was a steamy girl forbidden by the society in which I lived to make love. Perhaps because I was lucky enough also to have plenty of good writing at my disposal, the romantic novels did not make a romantic lover of me: it was only the 'nyum-nyum' sensations I needed, and I gave no more credence to their soppy message than a young child gives to a rabbit's little blue coat. Or than I myself gave to the Holy Trinity, first met at a time when I had taken my fill of baby-stories about animals and before I had begun to hunger for the sexy taste of romances, when I was just starting to feel my appetite for real life.

5

S o HERE I go, into advanced old age, towards my inevitable and no longer distant end, without the 'support' of religion and having to face the prospect ahead in all its bald reality. What are my feelings about that? I turn for enlightenment to the people I know who have gone ahead of me.

Most of the women on both sides of my family live into their nineties, keeping their wits about them. None of them has ever had to go into an old person's home, or has even had to employ live-in carers. All the married ones outlived their husbands and had daughters to see them through their last days, and the few who did their dying in hospital were there for only a day or two. I have become sharply aware of how lucky we have been in that respect, since the old age and death of my closest friend has taught me how much it costs to employ skilled home nursing, or to take refuge in a 'home' with staff as kind and understanding as they are efficient (no such place exists but some are nearer to it than others, usually because they cost hair-raising sums). No one in my family could have afforded either alternative for more than a week or so. What everyone wants is to live until the end in their own home, with the companionship of someone they love and trust. That is what my lot wanted and achieved, including my widowed mother, although I still feel guilty at the knowledge that in her case this happy conclusion was achieved by a narrow squeak.

By the time she was ninety-two I was seventy. She was deaf, blind in one eye and depending on a contact lens for sight in the other, so arthritic in her hips that she could hardly walk, and in her right arm that it was almost useless. She also had angina (still mild and infrequent) and vertigo (horribly trying and not infrequent). I was living in London, still by great good luck working, sharing a flat with an old friend who had barely enough money to cover his keep, while I had never earned enough to save a penny. Nothing would have made my mother confess that she longed to have me at home with her in Norfolk, but I knew that she did, and I believed that if you are the child of a loving, reliable and generously undemanding woman you owe her this consolation in her last years. I think that for people to look after their children when they are young, and to be looked after by them when they are old, is the natural order of events – although stupid or perverse parents can dislocate it. My mother was not stupid or perverse.

I ought, of course, to have seen to it that in the past I was paid what was due to me for my skills so that I could have bought a house in which, eventually, I could have accommodated my mother, instead of continuing in a small flat which an extraordinarily generous cousin let me have for a peppercorn rent.

Foreseeing my mother's old age, I did once raise the matter with André Deutsch (who was justified in taking more out of our firm than he allowed me because without him it would not have existed, but who allowed the discrepancy to become too great, being unable to resist taking advantage of my idiocy about money. No doubt if I had kicked and screamed I could have brought him to heel, but I was too lazy to face the hassle.) He thought, as usual, that the firm could not afford to increase my salary, but he consulted a money-wise friend who said that if I could find a suitable house, he could arrange for an insurance company to buy it, whereupon I could occupy it while I lived on advantageous terms which I have now forgotten. I found a charming little house with a surprisingly large garden and a ground floor which could become a flat for my mother, but the insurance company's surveyor declared it a bad risk because it was at the end of a row and had a bulge. It did not have even a hint of a bulge, nor has it now, a great many years later (I look carefully whenever I pass it), but I was not unwilling to be discouraged. Given support in this sensible project I would have pursued it happily enough, but without support my underlying reluctance to change my congenial way of life won the day, and I failed to look for another house.

And that is where the guilt is. There was a real, financial reason why it would have been unwise to give up my job and my London life; but no doubt my mother and I could have managed if we had absolutely had to. The reason was not as compelling as my strong disinclination to do so.

I was being no more selfish than my mother had been when her mother, at the age of ninety-four, was approaching death. My mother wanted to visit my sister in Southern Rhodesia, as it then was. Ought she to postpone the visit, given Gran's condition? She asked herself the question, then reported that Aunt Joyce, who lived with Gran and was carrying the full weight of her illness, had agreed that the postponement might alarm Gran by betraying that she was expected to die. I knew this was rationalization: that my mother was terrified of being there for the death and was hoping it would happen in her absence, as it did. All her life she had been the spoilt youngest daughter, the wilful one who could get away with things, unlike her responsible elders. I felt ashamed for her – perhaps even shocked – but not able to blame her. I was not seeing much of her at the time and thought I was free of family dependency, but that uncanny genetic closeness which forces one to feel in one's nerves what one's nearest kin are feeling in theirs was at work. And I am still unable to make her selfishness then feel like an excuse for my own.

Finally, however, the discomfort of guilt became too much for me, so I decided on a compromise between my disinclination to uproot and what I couldn't help seeing as my duty. I decided to spend four days – the weekend and a shopping day – with my mother for every three days in London, shuttling by car in good weather and by rail when the roads threatened to be bad. She had people to keep an eye on her during the week: Eileen Barry, a home help kind and reliable far beyond the call of duty, every morning; Sid Pooley, who chopped logs and did rough work in the garden every afternoon, while his wife Ruby mowed the lawns, picked and arranged flowers, and kept the bird-table supplied; and Myra, who cooked her supper, did her washing and ironing, and shopped for her (though rarely to my mother's satisfaction because, naturally enough, she bought things at shops she would visit anyway while catering for her family, and they were not to my mother's taste). At that time, in the country, such unprofessional but reliable help was not expensive – indeed, the home help was supplied free by the social services (this, I hear, has been discontinued).

Having announced my four-nights/three-nights plan I returned to London and collapsed into bed feeling horribly ill, with a temperature so low that I thought the thermometer must be broken; but once that involuntary protest was over I hit my stride, becoming quite good at suspending my life, which is what has to be done when living with an old person. You buy and cook the food that suits her, eat it at her set mealtimes, work in the garden according to her instructions, put your own work aside, don't listen to music because her hearing aid distorts it, and talk almost exclusively about her interests. She is no longer able to adapt to other people's needs and tastes, and you are there to enable her to indulge her own. Luckily gardening, my mother's great passion, is genuinely an interest of mine, and so is making things. All she could make by then, because of limited eyesight and rheumatic hands, was knitted garments, but her knitting was adventurous and I truly enjoyed discussing whether purple should be introduced, or a new pattern embarked on for the yoke. While my mother was well there was real pleasure in seeing her contented, and knowing she was more fully so because of my presence.

But she was not always well. Sometimes she went grey in the face and quietly slipped one of her 'heart pills' under her tongue; more often she had a less dangerous but more distressing attack of vertigo. She was clever at keeping her medicaments for this in strategic places, so that whether a 'dizzy' came on in the drawing room, the kitchen, her bedroom or the bathroom she could get herself without too much trouble into a chair with the necessary equipment. But gradually the length and intensity of the attacks increased, and the occasions on which I was thankful that I had been there to help her became more frequent. This did not lessen my anxiety at the prospect of such crises – indeed, it increased. If I woke during the night worry would start to nag, and I could rarely go to sleep again. I knew her usual movements very well: how she almost always shuffled along to the lavatory at about four in the morning (only the most acute emergency could make her use the commode I persuaded her to keep in her bedroom); how she began the slow process of washing and dressing at about six-thirty. If I didn't hear these sounds . . . was it because I had missed them, or was something wrong? I would have to get up and check. If I heard her cough, was it just an ordinary cough or was it the first retching of a vertigo? I had to listen tensely until its nature became clear. The anxiety seemed nearer to some kind of animal panic than anything rational. After all, I knew that I could help her through a vertigo, and even supposing it were a heart attack and she died of it, I knew that this sooner-rather-than-later inevitable event would be the timely conclusion of a long and good life, not a tragedy. But still, the way she was a little older, a little more helpless, a little more battered by that wretched vertigo with every week that passed – the fact that death was, so to speak, up in the attic of her house, waiting to come down and do something cruelly and fatally painful to her – frightened me.

I had been observing the four-night/three-night plan for about a year before I realized quite how much it frightened me. Of course it was tiring, even without the worry. I was working hard on my London days, so I never had time to be on my own and do my own things in my own home. I began to feel heavily weary. I drove to work every day, leaving my car in a garage about fifteen minutes walk away from the office – a pleasant walk, taking me through Russell Square, which I had always enjoyed. Now it began to seem exhausting; my feet seemed less manageable than they ought to be so I had to be careful not to stumble; I even began to dread it. And one weekend with my mother I felt so bad-tempered, so dreary, so near to irrational tears, that I decided I must see my doctor as soon as I got home. High blood pressure, he said: very much too high. This was both alarming and a relief: alarming because I had a secret dread of having a stroke, a relief because there was a real reason for feeling lousy, it was not just my imagination. The doctor said it was not surprising that I was suffering from stress and that I must take a proper holiday, and I added a scold to myself about my weight, which I hadn't bothered to check for months: it had gone up to twelve and a half stone! So my sister kindly came over from Zimbabwe for five weeks to be with my mother, and I stayed in my own dear bed for a week, then went for a week to a luxurious health clinic to start the process of weight-loss (successfully continued on my own). Once my blood pressure was back to normal and I was feeling well again – better than I had felt for years – I decided that I would not go on with the unbroken four/three plan, but would keep every third weekend to myself in London. This made sense, but it renewed guilt. In London I was able to shrug off anxiety and think about my own concerns (even enjoy them more than I used to because of having had to turn my back on them), but the night-time worries when I was staying with my mother were sharper than ever.

'I am not afraid of death.' My mother said this, and showed that she really was less afraid than many people by the calm way she discussed what would happen once she was gone. I believe the same is true of myself – but there are words which follow that statement so often that they have become a cliché: 'It's dying that I'm afraid of.' When dying is actually in sight, those words become shockingly true. My mother was not afraid of being dead, but when an attack of angina made her unable to breathe she was very frightened indeed. I was not afraid of her being dead, but I was terrified of the process of her dying.

I had seen only one dead person – and what a ridiculous state of affairs that was: that a woman in her seventies should have seen only one cadaver! Surely there has never been a taboo more senseless than our modern one on death. My only dead person was André Deutsch's ninety-two-year-old mother, who was found dead by her home help when André happened to be abroad. After the police had her body carried off to the coroner's mortuary they tracked down André's secretary and me and asked if one of us would identify the body. We decided to do it together.

On the way to the mortuary I recalled various reassuring descriptions of dead bodies: how they seemed empty and nothing to do with the person who had left them, and how beautiful faces become in the austere serenity of death. I wanted reassurance because I expected us to be in the same room as the body and to stand beside it while an attendant turned back a sheet covering its face, but that was not how it was done. We were taken into a narrow room with a large plate-glass window curtained with cheap sage-green damask. The curtain was drawn back and there was the body on the other side of the glass, lying in a box and covered up to the neck with a kind of bedspread of purple velour.

The words I spoke involuntarily were: 'Oh *poor* little Maria!' It did not look as though it had nothing to do with her, nor was it austerely serene. What was lying there was poor little Maria with her hair in a mess and her face grubby, looking as though she were in a state of great bewilderment and dejection because something too unkind for words had been done to her. It was a comfort to remember that she was dead, and therefore couldn't possibly be feeling how she looked. But it was not a comfort to be shown so clearly that my favourite image of floating out to sea at night was nonsense. What Maria's body demonstrated was that even a quick dying can be *very nasty*.

In other ways the coroner's domain was surprisingly bracing. We approached it through a walled yard where white vans with their rear windows painted out were coming and going. One of them was backed up close to a small unloading bay. It might have been delivering groceries, but was in fact delivering a body. The men who drove, loaded and unloaded the vans, several of whom were drinking tea in a room off the passage through which we entered, were middle-aged to elderly and looked tough and slightly ribald. They glanced at us sideways as we passed the door of their room, and in their eyes was the faintest hint – an almost imperceptible gleam – of mockery. *They knew.* They knew that however nasty death may be while it is happening, it is too ordinary an event to make a fuss about. Most of them, no doubt, went about their work soberly, but that hint of a gleam suggested that some of them might enjoy doing some flippancy to a corpse – using its navel as an ash-tray, perhaps – imagining as they did it the horror of a squeamish observer. They would probably respect the grief of the bereaved, but squeamishness they would despise. Having shed it, they had moved into a category apart.

My own reaction to this place where dead bodies were all in the day's work had something prurient about it. If the men in the room off the entrance passage looked at me out of the corners of their eyes, so did I at them: I did not want to betray the extent of my curiosity, did not want to be caught at it. My awareness of the cadavers hidden in the white vans and in the accommodation specially designed for them on Maria's side of the plate-glass window, was sharp. Had I been a dog my ears would have been pricked and my hackles up. I think this odd excitement was connected at some level with the violent recoil from dead animals which seized me in childhood when I unexpectedly came on a decaying corpse hidden in long grass, or caught in a trap, or on one of those macabre game-keeper's 'larders', the wires on which they strung up the corpses of 'vermin' they had trapped or shot. I often went a long way round to avoid passing one of those – in fact I think they are the reason why I have never much enjoyed walking through a wood. The two reactions seem like opposites, but could be the opposite sides of the same coin. Whatever the truth, I did call up that mortuary and those dead animals when trying to reason myself out of the night terrors in my mother's house: 'Calm down, this is not a matter of the mind saying "Alas, she will soon be dead and gone" – to that there is a whole set of other reactions of quite a different kind. This is simply a matter of flesh shuddering because flesh rots, and it is possible not only to acknowledge the ordinariness of that dissolution, but also to feel it.' Not long afterwards I wrote a poem – or perhaps more accurately a short statement – as a result of that visit to the mortuary, which had contributed a good deal to my attitude towards death.

I have learnt to recognize the plain white vans with painted-
    out back windows
and the black ones, equally discreet, standing at those back-
    street doors
which have a never-opened look (misleading).

The white vans carry dead junkies picked up in alleys, old
    women
found frozen when the neighbours began to wonder and called
    the cops,
the man who stayed late at his office to hang himself, the boy
stabbed in a sudden brawl outside a disco.

The black vans, early every morning, deliver coffins to
   mortuaries.

Men who handle corpses despise people who don't.
Why? How? What? Where? cry the hearts of the bereaved,
and the men who handle corpses lower their eyelids over
looks of secret but impatient ribaldry.
A few of them are necrophiliacs onto a good thing, but most
are normal men who have learnt from handling death
that it tells nothing because it has nothing to tell, there is
   nothing to it.

When I first recognized those vans I waited for my skin to
   crawl.
I am still surprised that they cheer me up.
'There goes death' I think when I see one. 'There it goes about
   its daily work,
and they think I don't see it. They think they are the only ones
with the nerve to know how ordinary it is.'

Recognition of a van: no more familiarity than that,
and already the look I give my unrecognizing friend
has in it, I suspect, a touch of secret but impatient ribaldry

When the time came for my mother to die, she was almost unbe-
lievably lucky – and therefore I was, too. On the day before her
ninety-sixth birthday she walked on her two sticks down to the end

of her garden, to oversee the planting of a new eucalyptus tree by Sid Pooley. Halfway through the planting he thought she looked not quite herself. 'Are you all right?' he asked, and she said she was feeling a bit unsteady and had better go back to the house. He helped her back, settled her in her chair, and called Eileen Barry, her home help, who came at once and recognized heart failure when she saw it. Eileen got her to the local cottage hospital and called me – by then it was 8.30 in the evening – saying it would probably be a good thing if I got there first thing next morning: no, she didn't think it was necessary for me to come straight away. I reached the hospital very early and found that my brother and my mother's favourite niece, both of whom lived fairly near, were already there. Soon after her death I again wrote a kind of poem describing it, which seems to me to belong here.

THE GIFT

It took my mother two days to die, the first of them cruel
as her body, ninety-five years old, crashed beyond repair.
I found her, 'an emergency' behind screens in a crowded ward,
jaw dropped, tongue lolling, eyes unseeing.
Unconscious? No. When about to vomit she gasped 'Basin!'
She was aware of what she was having to endure.

I put my hand on hers. Her head shifted, eyelids heaved up.
Her eyes focused.
Out of deep in that dying woman came a great flash
of recognition and of utmost joy.

My brother was there. Later he said,
'That was a very beautiful smile she gave you.'
It was the love I had never doubted flaming into visibility.
I *saw* what I had always believed in.

Next morning: quietness, sleep,
intervals of murmured talk.
'She is better!'
'She is feeling much better,' said the kind nurse,
'but she is still very very ill.'
I understood the warning and that what seemed miracle was
    morphine.

What did I feel? Like Siamese twins, one wanting her never to
    die,
the other dismayed at the thought of renewed life,
of having to go on dreading pain for her, go on foreseeing
her increasing helplessness and my guilt
at not giving up my life to be with her all the time.
What I felt was bad at being in two minds; but only for a while,
    because
perched in my skull above this conflict there was a referee
saying, 'Neither of you can win so shut up
and get on with doing whatever comes next.'

Her collapsed body eased, she was disconcerting to be with
because so alive.

On the edge of ceasing to exist
there she was, herself, tired but perfectly ordinary,
telling me what to do with her dog and where to find her will.
When my cousin protested 'But you'll soon be back home' she
    was cross.
'Don't be absurd,' she said, 'I could go any minute.'

Then, after a long sleep, she turned her head a little and said,
'Did I tell you that last week Jack drove me
to the nursery garden, to buy that eucalyptus?'
I too loved that garden and the drive through country
we had both known all our lives.
'You told me he was going to,' I said. 'Was it fun?'

She answered dreamily – her last words before sleeping again
out of which sleep she didn't wake:
'It was absolutely divine.'

Now that I am only seven years younger than my mother when she died, to what extent am I either supported by what I have learnt about dying, or made apprehensive about it? I have received a good deal of reassurance of a slightly wobbly kind, and also a cause for worry.

The reassurance concerns the actual process of dying. There cannot be many families in which so many people have been lucky in this respect as mine has been. Even the least lucky were spared the worst horrors of it (which can, of course and alas, be very bad). My maternal grandmother had to endure several months of distressing bedridden feebleness owing to prolonged heart failure, but she had a daughter to help her through it at home and that daughter was able to report that the attack which finally killed her was a good deal less disagreeable than some of those that she survived. My father had to endure one week that was certainly horrible, though no one could be sure how aware he was of its horribleness: he had a cerebral haemorrhage which deprived him of speech and left him obviously extremely confused. Once settled in hospital he could respond normally when offered a basin to wash in or a meal to eat, and when you came into his room he looked pleased to see you and attempted to speak; but he could find no words and an expression of distress followed by hopelessness appeared on his face. I got the impression that he knew something was dreadfully wrong, was miserable about it, then thought, 'Oh well, it seems I can't do anything about it so I'd better stop trying.' The doctor saw no possibility of repair to the damage, but found him physically strong, which was alarming: my mother and I couldn't bring ourselves to speak about the possibility of his living for a long time in this condition. But a second haemorrhage struck, killing him instantly, and whatever he was aware of suffering during the intervening days, there were only six of them.

About the deaths of my paternal grandparents, my father's siblings and my mother's father I know little, but nothing was ever said to suggest that they were particularly harrowing, while on my mother's side one sister had a stroke when she was eighty-three from which she died almost at once without recovering consciousness; another aged ninety-four was distressed for less than an hour, then died in a daughter's arms just after saying that she was now feeling much better; another went quietly after becoming increasingly weak and dozy for about three weeks; and their brother, a lucky man whose luck held to the very end, was on his horse at a meet of the Norwich Stag-hounds at the age of eighty-two, talking with friends, when flop! and he fell off his horse stone dead in the middle of a laugh. The eldest of my cousins had similar luck, falling down dead as she was making a cup of tea.

My brother, who died last year, was less lucky, but not because he was painfully ill for a long time, or afraid of death. His trouble was that he resented it because he loved his life so passionately. He was eighty-five. He knew death was coming because, having stubbornly refused to pay attention to various ailments of old age which were obvious to his anxious wife and other people, he was finally forced to recognize that his appetite had gone and that he was feeling dreadfully cold. But he still longed to be out messing about with his boats – he lived on the Norfolk coast in a place he adored and to have to leave that place and its occupations seemed to him the worst possible fate.

One afternoon not long before he died he took me out for a sail. His house is just inland from Blakeney Point, a long spit of sand dunes that runs parallel to the shore, partially enclosing a stretch of water which at low tide becomes a river snaking its way out to sea through exposed mud, but at high tide is a wide, sheltered expanse busy with small sailing boats and easily navigated by larger ones provided they are careful to observe the markers showing where the deeper channels run. On that day there was hardly a breath of wind. Sky and water were mother-of-pearl and the breasts of doves, a blend of soft blues and pinks so delicate that I had never seen its like. A small group of sailing dinghies was lying becalmed, hoping to be able to start a race (we, who were motoring, gave one of them which had no outboard engine a tow to join the group). None of the people lounging at the tiller of these little boats looked impatient or bored, because no one could mind being becalmed in the middle of so much loveliness. When we were some way past them, near the end of the Point, almost in the open sea, a tiny popple began under our hull and and a cat's paw of breeze – a kitten's paw, more like it – just ruffled the water's surface enough for sunlight to start twinkling off the edges of each ripple; I was once told that fishermen at Aldeburgh used to call that effect of light 'tinkling cymbals'. I shall always think of it as that, and no tinkling cymbals I ever saw were better than those we moved through when Andrew was at last able to hoist canvas and very, very gently we started to sail. We didn't talk much. Although we didn't often see each other and differed widely in many of our opinions, he and I had never lost touch with the closeness we had enjoyed in early childhood and there was much that we could understand about each other without words. That afternoon was brimming with a loveliness peculiar to that particular place; he knew that I was appreciating it, and I knew without any doubt how profoundly he was penetrated by it. He was a man who, with the help of the right wife, had finally found himself the place and the life that fulfilled him, and lived it with a completeness and intensity more often seen in an artist than in someone who should have been a farmer, had to become an army officer, and ended by teaching people sailing, and growing oysters, on the edge of the North Sea. What filled him as death approached was not fear of whatever physical battering he would have to endure (in fact there was not, at the end, any of that), but grief at having to say goodbye to what he could never have enough of.

Such a grief, it seems to me, is proof of a good, or at least an agreeable, life, and ought therefore to be something for which one is grateful – provided, of course, that one has not been cut off untimely, and I know that my brother agreed with me that once past eighty one has no right to complain about dying, because he said so. I guess that if I am given the time for it, I too shall feel at least a little of it, and hope to remember that it is simply what one has to pay for what one has enjoyed.

So: I have inherited a good chance of going fairly easily, and I have found it easy to think myself into a reasonable attitude towards death. It is not surprising, therefore, that I spend no time worrying about it. When I worry, it is about living with the body's failures, because experience has shown me that when that ordeal is less hard than it might have been, it is usually because of the presence of a daughter. And I have no daughter. Barry, the person closest to me – we became lovers sixty-three years ago and started sharing this flat eight years later – has beaten me to physical collapse, so that I have to look after him. And I haven't got the money to pay for care of any kind. If I don't have the luck to fall down dead while still able-bodied, as my uncle and my cousin did (and that luck certainly can only be hoped for, not counted on), it is going to be the geriatric ward for me.

Fortunately, if a prospect is bleak enough the mind jibs at dwelling on it. It's not a matter of *choosing* not to think about it, more of *not being able* to do so. Whatever happens, I will get through it somehow, so why fuss? Now that I have attempted to assess my own attitude, that seems to be it. Those last miserable weeks or months (may it not be years!) when you are unable to look after yourself are so disagreeable anyway that it hardly matters how they are spent. My oldest friend died this year, my age, daughterless like me but with enough money first for carers visiting her home, then for a nursing home reckoned to be an exceptionally good one, which given what it cost it damn well should have been. From time to time, in emergencies, she also had to spend a week or so in hospital, in wards full of other ancient people, and she didn't seem to be any unhappier there than she was in the expensive 'home'. The one real drawback to a ward, I felt, was that the nursing was better there so they were more likely to haul you back from the brink to suffer further misery than they were at the 'home'. She, on the other hand, was always glad when hauled back. Perhaps when one comes to it one always is? By the time I've learnt whether that is true for me I shall be past handing on the news.

That is all I have to say about the event of death and what I feel about it in advance, so now I shall move on – or perhaps 'over' is more exact – to the experience of living during one's last years.

WHAT HAPPENS TODAY is, of course, closely interwoven with what happened yesterday, being simply a continuation of the same process: only those old people afflicted with senile dementia move on to another plane. For the rest of us, as we have sown, so do we reap. And one of the best parts of my harvest comes from a lucky piece of sowing a long time ago.

Soon after the event described on page 24, when I first had to accept the fact that I was on the wane sexually, Barry Reckord, my lover-turned-just-friend, decided to take a play of his, *White Witch*, to Jamaica. All but one of the people in the play are Jamaicans, so those parts could be cast when he got there, but the 'witch' herself is English, so her interpreter had to be found here and taken with him. He couldn't afford an established actor, so it had to be someone young and inexperienced who was going to be offered the thrill of this big and juicy part, and who would probably be excited enough by it to take off happily for several months in the Caribbean on very little money.

Almost the first he auditioned was a farmer's daughter from Somerset, Sally Cary, who read the part well and was pretty enough for it, although to my mind her looks ought to have been a touch more extreme and eccentric. Barry liked them, however, and judged (rightly) that she would be capable of expressing the part's character once on stage. So off they went, and the production was successful. I was not surprised when it became apparent from Barry's letters that he and Sally had slipped into an affair.

When they got back to England I was, however, slightly surprised to see how serious it was – certainly very far from being a passing flutter. But that was explained almost at once. Barry and I are similar in our responses to intelligence, honesty and generosity, so when it turned out that Sally was one of the nicest young women – one of the nicest people – I had ever met, I had no trouble understanding why he loved her. Certainly if I had still been in a physical relationship with him it would have pained me to see them together, but because by then I had fully acknowledged within myself that sex between us was gone for good, it didn't worry me. It was a great piece of luck that this important shift in our relationship had happened before Sally came into our lives.

She found herself a bedsitter not far from us, and returned to the nerve-racking routine of auditions, getting work so rarely that paying for her room was not easy. Her parents, though both from farming families as well as being farmers themselves, had apparently begun to resent the rigours of their life enough to want to rescue their three daughters from it. The two elder girls had married Americans, and Sally, with her good contralto voice and gift for acting, had been firmly pointed towards a career on the stage. She said that her father positively discouraged her from taking an interest in the farm, and she really seemed to know little about it: I used to tease her for not knowing the difference between wheat and barley. From school she went on to an acting school, and she was still taking singing lessons.

Quite soon it occurred to me that, since she was spending almost every night in Barry's bed, keeping on her bedsitter was a waste of money, so I suggested that she should move in with us. It seemed to me that I would enjoy having her with us, and so I did. I know people thought our *ménage à trois* odd, though whether I acquired undeserved merit for generosity, or disapproval for loose morals, I could never tell because no one was ever impolite enough to comment. I suspect there was more of the former than the latter, given that no one could live through the 1960s without at least hearing possessiveness condemned, even if they didn't condemn it themselves. It is true that many people are so neurotically possessive that they can't bear seeing someone enjoying something even if they don't want it for themselves, but I was not, and still am not, possessive like that, not because I had trained myself out of it but simply because I wasn't made that way – luck, not virtue, for which I am grateful, having often witnessed the miseries of jealousy. When Sally joined us what I felt was that now I had a lovely new friend in the house, as well as a darling old one, and the next two years or so were some of the happiest I can remember.

That stage came to an end when Sally's father's health deteriorated. She had already given up singing lessons (her teacher had said she ought to write I WANT TO BE THE BEST CONTRALTO IN THE WORLD and stick it up above her mirror, and she had thought, 'How bloody silly! I don't in the least want to be the best contralto in the world'); and although she enjoyed acting she was not obsessed by it and detested the often humiliating ordeal of auditions. She therefore came to the conclusion that she ought to go home and help her father, to which end she signed up for a course on farm management at Cirencester. I think I missed her almost as much as Barry did, but by that time friendship had consolidated into a sense of belonging together like family, so that there was no question of 'losing' her, not even when at Cirencester she met Henry Bagenal and they decided to get married. Henry, being a warm-hearted and wise young man very much liked by both Barry and me, simply joined the family, so to speak. On Mr Cary's death the two of them took over the farm, and when Jessamy and Beauchamp were born it was almost as though Barry had acquired two grandchildren, and me too to a slightly lesser degree.

So now, in my old age, although I have not in fact got a daughter and grandchildren, I *have* got people who are near to filling those roles. One of the most impressive things about Sally has been that although she didn't seem to be unusually drawn to children before she married, once she had them she opened out into motherhood with astonishing completeness, yet without losing herself. She was, for instance, determined to breastfeed her babies and to go on doing so until they chose to give it up. Jessamy, her first child, continued to return to the breast when she needed to be comforted well into her third year, by which time she could understand and agree that it must be passed on to her little brother because he couldn't do without it while she could. All the usual arguments had been brought to bear on Sally – it was unnecessary, it was indecent, it would tie her down, it would wear her out, and above all it would make the child neurotically dependent on her – and she had disregarded them. What in fact happened was that conveniently portable Jess was absorbed into adult life instead of imprisoning her mother in the nursery, then developed into a child so secure that her self-confidence and independence were remarkable, and has now become a young adult who leaves us all gaping with admiration and envy as she sails triumphantly into her career as a doctor, living – to our great good luck – in a flat five minutes' walk from us. And her brother Beachy, in his very different way, is equally beautiful and successful, while their mother, who has never for a moment failed either of them and is as much loved as she is loving, simultaneously built herself a full-time career in the organic food movement. Her two children are far from being the only remarkably attractive young people of my close acquaintance – I have nephews, nieces, great-nephews and great-nieces, all of whom make nonsense of gloomy forebodings about modern youth – but they are the two I see most often, so it is they who seem to symbolize my good fortune in this respect.

What is so good about it is not just the affection young people inspire and how interesting their lives are to watch. They also, just by being there, provide a useful counteraction to a disagreeable element in an old person's life. We tend to become convinced that everything is getting worse simply because within our own boundaries things *are* doing so. We are becoming less able to do things we would like to do, can hear less, see less, eat less, hurt more, our friends die, we know that we ourselves will soon be dead . . . It's not surprising, perhaps, that we easily slide into a general pessimism about life, but it is very boring and it makes dreary last years even drearier. Whereas if, flitting in and out of our awareness, there are people who are *beginning*, to whom the years ahead are long and full of who knows what, it is a reminder – indeed it enables us actually to feel again – that we are not just dots at the end of thin black lines projecting into nothingness, but are parts of the broad, many-coloured river teeming with beginnings, ripenings, decayings, new beginnings – are still parts of it, and our dying will be part of it just as these children's being young is, so while we still have the equipment to see this, let us not waste our time grizzling.

And if we are lucky enough, as I am, to be from time to time in quite close contact with young people, they can sometimes make it easier to hang on to this notion when they function, as every person does vis-à-vis every other person they come up against, as a mirror.

Always we are being reflected in the eyes of others. Are we silly or sensible, stupid or clever, bad or good, unattractive or sexy . . . ? We never stop being at least slightly aware of, if not actively searching for, answers to such questions, and are either deflated or elated, in extreme cases ruined or saved, by what we get. So if when you are old a beloved child happens to look at you as if he or she thinks (even if mistakenly!) that you are wise and kind: what a blessing! It's not that such a fleeting glimpse of yourself can convert you into wiseness and kindness in any enduring way; more like a good session of reflexology which, although it can cure nothing, does make you feel like a better person while it's going on and for an hour or two afterwards, and even that is well worth having.

The more frequent such shots of self-esteem are, the more valuable they become, so there is a risk – remote, but possible – of their becoming addictive. An old person who doesn't enjoy having young people in her life must be a curmudgeon, but it is extremely important that she should remember that risk and watch her step. Or he, his. Not long ago I sat at dinner next to a lively man in his late sixties or early seventies who announced blithely that he got on very well with young people, he didn't know why but they seemed to feel as though he were the same age as they were. And as he spoke his intelligent face slid into a fatuous smile. Oh, you poor dear! is what I felt. Then – it was unkind of me, and almost certainly useless – I told a little story from my own experience.

When I was eighteen or nineteen we were all surprised to learn that a man who lived near us had got married. It had been assumed that he was a confirmed bachelor because he had reached the age of (I think) forty-nine as an apparently contented single man, a condition attributed to his dimness, not to any suspicion of his being gay. People were pleased for him when they learnt that he had found a wife, a suitable woman in her mid-forties, but there was a touch of amusement in the way they discussed it. There had been enough talk about it for me to be interested when I went to a dance and saw them there, just back from their honeymoon. I watched them take to the floor together, two small, sandy-haired, plain but cheerful-looking *old people* – no, more than cheerful-looking, rapturously happy. They were glowing. They were gazing into each other's eyes. They had shut their eyes and were dancing cheek pressed to cheek. *And it was disgusting.* 'I suppose,' I thought, 'that old people must still make love [in those days it didn't occur to us to say fuck], but they ought to have the decency not to show it.' And I was a kind, well brought-up girl who would not have dreamt of betraying that response if I had been face to face with them.

It does seem to me that the young nowadays are often more sophisticated than I used to be, and that many of them – certainly my own darlings – relate to their elders more easily than we did; but I am convinced that one should never, never *expect* them to want one's company, or make the kind of claims on them that one makes on a friend of one's own age. Enjoy whatever they are generous enough to offer, and leave it at that.

As well as relationships there are, of course, activities, which are almost as important. There was a time, about twenty years ago, when if you lived in London it was possible to take, almost for free, evening classes in a vast number of subjects. For years I had felt snobbishly that such activities were not for me, but when I became too fat to find ready-made clothes I liked in any shop I could afford, it occurred to me that I might learn dress-making, so I made enquiries and my eyes were opened. I was awe-struck, when I went to the local primary school in order to enrol in a dress-making class, to discover how many subjects were offered: painting, several kinds of dancing, plumbing, languages including Chinese, Russian and Latin, motor mechanics, antique collecting – you named it and you could learn it. So soon a group of us were crouched like gnomes at tiny desks in the infants' library every Wednesday evening, stitching merrily away. We were probably uncommonly lucky in having dear Biddy Maxwell for our tutor, who not only taught us very well, but also became the central figure in a cluster of friendships that endures to this day, but it seemed obvious that we were not the only class having a good time.

About six years later this abundance of almost-free classes began to shrivel. It had started to be under threat a bit earlier: if fewer than ten people turned up at any class it was closed down, so from time to time we had to hijack an obliging husband, give him a scrap of material and tell him to look as though he were making himself a tie. But finally the whole of that particular system ended; though there still, of course, continued to be institutions running evening classes for those willing to pay, and as far as I was concerned classes for adults had become a welcome part of life.

It was my mother who first caused me to associate the idea of them with painting, because in her mid-seventies she had taken up Painting for Pleasure classes. Some of her fellow students were content with making careful copies of postcards, but some, among whom she was one of the bravest, were more adventurous. She produced many bold still lives and one quite startling self-portrait, and she enjoyed it very much, so when I reached my mid-seventies, and after dress-making had been closed down, it seemed natural to follow her example. I had always loved painting lessons at school, had once enjoyed a short fling as a Sunday painter before realizing that my job simply didn't allow me time for it, and was still aware that if I wanted to draw something I was able to make some kind of stab at it. I was still at work when I joined my first life class (I didn't retire until I was seventy-five), and soon realized that the necessary concentration called for more energy than, in those circumstances, I could command. But after I had retired I found an agreeable and well-equipped life class just round the corner from where I live, and that I continued for some time.

I think I was almost the only student in that class whose aim was to reproduce the appearance of the model. What most of the others seemed to aim for was marks on paper that gave what they hoped was the effect of modern art. To them my attempts must have seemed boring and fogeyish; to me theirs appeared an absurd waste of time, and I still think I was right. This may be because I am old, but being old doesn't necessarily make one wrong. I am pretty sure that it is not only the old who are unable to regard as art anything that does not involve the mastery of a skill.

Given a lot of money I would collect art, both drawings and paintings. There are many ways in which a painting can be exciting, but a drawing that thrills me is always one that has caught a moment of life. Drawings are what artists, great or small, do when they are working their way towards understanding something, or catching something they want to preserve: they communicate with such immediacy that they can abolish time. I possess a drawing by a Victorian artist of his wife teaching their little girl to read by candlelight; in a book about Pisanello, who lived in the fourteen-hundreds, I have four quick sketches he made of men who had been hung. Each, in its different way, makes one catch one's breath: one might be there, looking through the eyes of the men who did those drawings. (Perhaps oddly, drawings presented as works of art are less likely to have this hallucinatory effect than private notes or studies.)

Many people will never have hands and eyes that can collaborate in a way that allows them to draw. A few specially gifted people have them from the start. In some of us they don't work effectively to begin with, but might possibly be trained by practice – and surely the purpose of a life class is to do just that? It is to teach you how to look, and then how to make your hand reproduce what you are looking at, eventually with such confidence that the lines it draws are in themselves pleasing (or perhaps exhilarating, or scary, or whatever) as well as explanatory of the object drawn. Once that degree of skill has been achieved, off you can go and take as many liberties with appearances as you like; what you produce will never be inert.

It was only when I tried to draw a naked body that I began to see how difficult it is, and how important. When you have a naked person in front of you, calmly exposed to your concentrated study, you see how accurate the term 'life class' is. What you are looking at is precisely life, that inexplicable and astounding cause of our being, to which everything possible in the way of attention and respect is due. That is why most people find it more interesting to draw other people, or animals, or plants and trees, rather than man-made objects such as architecture or machinery. (There are, of course, fine draughtsmen who specialize in those – and no doubt it's a foolish quirk of mine that makes me suspect they will be bores.)

Since I first tried to draw a nude figure it has seemed to me that what determines the quality of a drawing is the attention and respect, rather than the ingenuity, that an artist has devoted to what he is looking at. One should become as skilful as possible in order to probe the true nature of the object one is studying.

An object, of course, is needed for such probing, or sometimes a subject embodied in objects – think of Goya's *Disasters of War* or his bullfighting sequence. To make a flat surface interesting to look at simply for its own sake – turn it into an artefact that will hold the attention, move and/or give pleasure to others as well as yourself, does naturally require gifts – you must understand colour and be inventive about pattern, which are not common abilities. But quite often what it chiefly seems to need is taking yourself very seriously. Only a person with a gigantic sense of self-importance could, for example, produce a large number of canvases painted in a single flat colour, or even in two or three flat colours, without being bored to death. That is the kind of non-representational art that strikes me as absurd. Other kinds can be very pleasing in the same kind of way as a good piece of interior decoration, but to me they do not grip, as works that probe, question, celebrate or attack a subject can grip.

Much as I enjoyed that second life class, I gave it up when I saw that only if I worked at it every day could I hope to draw better, and that even then, being a word person rather than an image person, I would never amount to more than an illustrator. I fear that it was a kind of vanity that caused me to lose interest once I was convinced that my best could never be better than second rate. I do still sometimes amuse myself by trying to draw, and wish I had the energy to do so more often because it remains an absorbing occupation. And however far from being an artist my feeble attempts have left me, I am grateful to those classes for one positive result: I am now much better at seeing things than I used to be. That is something often said by people who have tried to draw, and it is a good reason for making the attempt, even in old age, because it adds such a generous pinch of pleasure to one's days.

No less intensely than drawing, but much more consistently, gardening has been an activity which has given me, and still gives me, great pleasure. In my early youth it was something done for you by employees: a head gardener with two men under him in my maternal grandparents' household, and one man in ours – a full-time man to start with, becoming increasingly part-time as money dwindled. But even my grandmother, who certainly did no digging with her own hands, knew exactly what was happening in her garden and how and why it should be done. Certain things she always did herself: cut back the lavender, for instance, and spread it to dry on sheets so that the flowers could be rubbed off for lavender bags, which were kept with her linen; and spray her roses against greenfly with a big brass syringe which lived in the flower room (a little room with a sink where she arranged flowers for the house, and where the dogs slept). Her spray was nothing more lethal than a bucketful of soft soap dissolved in warm water, and the roses were always pristine. As children we loved the roses, watched eagerly for the first snowdrops, stroked the velvet of pansy petals, had our other favourite flowers, but the garden was not simply a place to be looked at. We *inhabited* it: climbed its trees, hid in its bushes, fished tadpoles and newts from its stream, stole its peaches and grapes (which was a sin and therefore more exciting that eating its plums and apples from the branch, which was allowed). And we were given regular tasks such as picking the sweet-peas for Gran and the strawberries and raspberries which were to come to the table that day. Towards the end of each season such tasks became a bit of a chore, but they were never disagreeable, and because they always involved delicious tastes and smells and pleasant leafy sensations, a garden was naturally accepted as a source of sensuous pleasure as well as a place full of beauty.

That was also true for my mother and her sisters before me (it was a family in which the women were more concerned with gardening than the men). All four of them became enthusiastic and knowledgeable gardeners, and they did more gardening work than their mother had done because none of them married a man as rich as their father. As I grew up, however, I moved away from my childhood and their continuing involvement. I went away, first to Oxford, then to London, and although on my visits home I appreciated the several gardens my mother made over the years, I looked at them rather than inhabited them, and I never worked in them. I never so much as pulled a weed or sowed a seed, and I became ignorant. Once, when I was staying with a friend who had just moved into a new house, she showed me a clump of leaves in a neglected flower bed which she wanted to restore, and asked what I thought they were. 'Pansies, I think,' said I; so we separated the clump and planted bits of it all along the front of the bed. And what those pansies turned out to be was Michaelmas daisies.

The London house, the top flat of which I moved into early in the 1960s and where I am still lucky enough to live, has a small front garden and a back one slightly larger than a tennis court. When my cousin Barbara bought the house the back garden consisted of a lawn with a fairly wide border the length of one side of it, an ivy-swamped raised border across the end, and a scramble of weeds that had once been a border next to the steps leading up to the lawn. The long border was full of still floriferous but very old and gnarled roses, which my cousin kept weeded and from time to time was nudged by her mother into pruning, but otherwise, apart from keeping the grass cut, she let the garden look after itself, which meant that the laurel bush and the fiercely thorny pyracanthus which grew against the wall opposite the rose bed grew almost to house height and plunged most of the space in shade. The lawn served a useful purpose, however, as a playground for her young children and a home for their guinea pigs, and that was what she minded about.

Twenty-six years ago her job took her to Washington, where she was to live for six or seven years, and it was agreed that I should find tenants for the bottom part of the house while the middle flat should be the preserve of her son, who was then at Oxford. Just before she left she asked me if I could 'sort of keep an eye' on the garden so that 'nature didn't quite take over'. And the next morning, leaning out of my bedroom window and surveying what had now become my territory, I suddenly and absolutely unexpectedly became my mother. 'There's only one thing for it,' I heard myself saying. 'I must take the whole thing out and start from scratch.' And that is what I did. I paid someone to do the heavy digging and cutting back, and for new brickwork in the front garden, but all the planting I did myself, and as soon as the first plant I put in with my own hands actually *grew and flowered*, I was hooked.

For a long time I spent most of my evenings and weekends working in that garden, which became quite adventurous and colourful, but gradually digging and mowing became too much for me, and about five years ago I reshaped it into something more sober which could be controlled by a gardening firm coming in once a fortnight – dull, but soothing to sit in on a summer evening – and lost interest in it, although I am still proud of the huge white rambling rose that submerges the crab-apple tree, the magnolia and the three other roses. But by then I had half an acre of garden in Norfolk to think about, *real* garden, rich in possibilities, belonging to the little house my cousin inherited from her mother in which she has generously granted me a share. She loves to sit in it, but is happy to let me run it, and building on my aunt's original creation is a continuing joy.

For some time now most of the work has to be done by other hands, so my cousin employs a young man who mows the lawn and keeps the hedges trimmed, while I have employed a sequence of three serious gardeners, all women, all much more knowledgeable than I am, and each in her different way a wonder-worker. I can afford help only one day a week, but what they have achieved! The first two did a tremendous amount of structural work, and my present treasure is a sophisticated plantswoman with whom I have a delightful time choosing what to plant where: to me the part of gardening that is the most fulfilling. And still, each time I'm there, I manage to do at least a little bit of work myself: tie something back, trim something off, clear some corner of weeds, plant three or four small plants, and however my bones may ache when I've done it, I am always deeply refreshed by it. Getting one's hands into the earth, spreading roots, making a plant comfortable – it is a totally absorbing occupation, like painting or writing, so that you become what you are doing and are given a wonderful release from consciousness of self. And so, for that matter, is simply sitting in your garden, taking it in. The following is from a short-lived diary I kept at a time when Barry was ill. I had not been able to get to Norfolk for two months, but now his brother had come to stay so I could snatch a weekend.

'Back here at last, and in exquisite spring weather, the narcissi full out with later ones still to come, the Japanese cherry by the gate a mass of pale lacy pinkness, the primroses exuberant, the magnolia opening, everything coming alive – intoxicating. However good this garden can be in summer, it's never better than now, thanks to nothing done by me but to the clever way Aunt Doro planted her bulbs in drifts years ago now expanded by their naturalization. This afternoon I sat for a long time by the pond, in the thick of them, trying to tell myself "Beauty is in the eye of the beholder, these starry green and gold creatures are just vegetable organisms shaped and coloured according to natural laws for reasons of survival. They don't exist for the sake of beauty any more than a nettle does" . . . but it was impossible to believe it. It might be true, but so what! I choose it to be untrue because the daffodils don't allow me to do otherwise.'

And still I can see those flowers in my mind's eye, serene beings, quietly living their own mysterious lives, and know that in a few months' time they will be back and with any luck I will be there again to see them . . . Yes, I am much the richer since Barbara asked me to keep an eye on her garden.

10

'WHEN I AM eighty-two I must start thinking about giving up the car.' That resolution, made in my early seventies, was the result of a visit made to my mother by her local policeman (we still had them then) when I happened to be staying with her. I opened the door to him, and he almost embraced me, so glad was he to find an intermediary for his embarrassing message. Could I please try to persuade my mother that the time had come for her to stop driving? No one had liked to say anything to her face, but three people in the village had told him that they had witnessed, or almost been the victim of, her driving, which had recently become . . . well, he didn't want to offend, but it *had* become a little bit erratic. I passed the message on, she dismissed it huffily as nonsense, and about six weeks later, much to my relief, announced, 'Oh, by the way – I have decided to get rid of the car.'

I now understand her reluctance only too well. While pottering about in the car hardly qualifies as an 'activity', it is – for those whose physical mobility is limited – a part of life and a source of pleasure. At a time when strictly speaking I ought to have followed her example by overcoming reluctance, I didn't do so. It was during my seventies when I should have stopped driving, because cataracts in both eyes developed to the point at which I could no longer read the number plate of a car three car-lengths ahead – indeed could hardly read one on a car immediately in front of me. But the licensing authority errs (quite rightly!) on the side of caution, because being unable to distinguish details within an object doesn't mean you can't see the object itself, and since I never suffered any uncertainty as to where or what any object, large or small, near or far, might be, I felt no serious guilt at continuing to drive up to the time of my operations.

André Deutsch, who believed firmly that the more something costs the better it must be, took it on himself to try to organize these operations and bullied me into seeing 'my wonderful man in Harley Street'. I saw him, and when he passed me on to his secretary so that I could make the appointment for the operation, thought to ask her how much it was going to cost. It would be done at the London Clinic, she said, where I would have to stay for two nights, 'so we will be looking at something like £3000'. So what in fact I looked at was the splendid if rather Dickensian-seeming Moorfields Eye Hospital, where the operations were done for free with exquisite precision, the first of them at about lunchtime so that I was home in time for supper, the second early in the morning so I was home in time for lunch. And the whole thing seemed like a glorious miracle because they assumed that I knew the nature of the modern operation, so didn't tell me in advance that they would not be simply removing the cataracts, but would also be giving me new eyes by inserting tiny permanent lenses designed to correct such faults as there had been in my sight before the cataracts began. I had been short-sighted all my life, and suddenly I could see like a hawk and no longer needed glasses, except for the readers that the 'long sight' of old age necessitates. Since then I have heard two or three sad stories of cataract operations which went wrong, but I remember my own with heartfelt gratitude.

When I turned eighty-two I remembered the resolution I had made and I did start thinking about whether or not I should give up my car, but all I could see was that while walking more than a quarter of a mile had become impossible, my driving showed no sign of being any different from what it always had been. Therefore I decided, 'No, not quite yet.' By now, six years on, I probably ought to think again. My legs have almost given out and I am hard put to it to walk a hundred yards. It started with painful feet – painful for the simple but incurable reason that the flesh padding their soles gradually becomes thinner and thinner until at last your poor old bones are grinding into the ground with every step. This leads to incorrect walking so that soon your knees are affected, and then your hips, until there comes a time when it dawns on you that your legs as a whole have become so useless that if you tried to depend on them for more than a few steps without some sort of prop such as sticks, or god help you a Zimmer, you would simply *fall down*. And at that point your car begins to represent life. You hobble towards it, you ease your unwieldy body laboriously into the driver's seat – and lo! you are back to normal. Off you whizz just like everyone else, restored to freedom, restored (almost) to youth. I always liked my car. Now I love it. But of course this increased love and dependence coincides with the deterioration of other things besides your legs, so the postponed 'thinking about it' *does* need to be done. At the time of writing this, which is precisely a month before my eighty-ninth birthday, I have to admit that my car does carry three scars acquired within the last year, after never having any to show apart from those inflicted on it by others because it lives on the street.

Scar one: a very slight dent on its backside made when I was parking in a space next to a skip and failed to allow for the fact that the top rim of the skip stuck out. Scar two: not really a scar at all because easily straightened out by hand, but my passenger-side mirror did hit something hard enough to be almost flattened against the car's side when, in a narrow street full of oncoming traffic, I failed to judge correctly how much room I had on that side. Scar three, and this one is bad: a scrape, slightly dented, far back on the driver's side, of which I am much ashamed. At the end of a long, traffic-choked drive, when it had become dark, I forgot that the gate into Hyde Park just past the Hyde Park Hotel in the direction of Hyde Park Corner has long been permanently closed, and turned into its entrance, thus trapping myself in a little stub of roadway ending at a shut gate, with cars parked on both its sides and a row of bollards down its middle. The space between the bollards was not wide and was ill-lit, so a U-turn was not going to be easy, but the unbroken stream of headlights roaring past behind me made the prospect of reversing out into it unthinkable, so the

U-turn it would have to be. I had nearly completed it when I felt the pressure of a bollard against the car's side. And what did I do? Instead of stopping at once, reversing and starting again at a wider angle, I thought 'If I go on it will make a nasty scrape – oh, what the hell, who cares!' and on I went. Which was wholly the result of being an overtired *old person* flustered by her own silliness in landing herself in an awkward situation.

But oddly enough I was not responsible for the worst accident I ever had – so bad that I still marvel at being alive – which happened earlier in this same year. The M11, where it bypasses Newmarket, has three lanes, and as with most three-lane motorways, the slow lane is so full of heavy vehicles travelling on the slow side of 70 m.p.h. that few cars use it, so in the other two lanes there is nothing to check the traffic from moving rather faster than it ought to, nearer to 80 m.p.h. than 70. I, on my familiar journey between London and Norfolk, was cheerfully buzzing along in the middle lane, not trying to overtake anything but simply going faster in the faster stream, and thus passing the heavy vehicles on my left. Just as my nose came level with the tail-end of one of them (not, thank god, one of the monsters), without having indicated its intention, it started to swing into the middle lane. Either I had to hit it, or I had to swerve into the fast lane. I can't say I made a decision, I didn't have time, I simply followed instinct and swerved. Whereupon crash! A car coming on fast in the fast lane hit me. For what seemed minutes but must have been only seconds I was sandwiched between the two vehicles, ricochetting from one to the other, then I suppose the lorry braked and the other vehicle pulled ahead. I had a flash of

'That's better!', then blank horror: my car had gone out of control and what I did with my steering wheel had become utterly irrelevant, I was spinning across the width of the motorway, zig, zag, whoosh, a complete pirouette, the shoulder coming towards me, grass, thank god it's grass, and there I was on it, facing the wrong way, and the traffic roared on. Not a single other vehicle had been touched.

The lorry didn't stop. The car that hit me did, and its driver's husband walked back – they had to go on some distance before being able to cross the traffic and park – to exchange addresses and insurance companies, and he was concerned and kind. By the time he reached me my greatest piece of luck (after surviving and not having caused a god-awful pile-up) had brought me an ambulance driver and his mate, who had been coming on behind and had seen the whole thing. They not only stopped, but called the police for me and then stayed with me until they came, a long half-hour. 'Someone up there is watching out for you,' said the driver in an awe-struck voice. He also said I'd handled it well, but really all I'd done was hung on grimly and refrained from braking. It was a baking hot day, the roar and stink of the traffic was hideous, and I can't think how, in my state of shock, I would have got through that half-hour on that narrow shoulder without the presence of those two kind men. I am still miserable at the fact that because I was in shock it never occurred to me to ask for their names and addresses.

After the first policeman arrived I slowly became able to see in a distant kind of way that it was becoming funny. He took a statement from the ambulance driver, which spared me from having to attempt a description, then said that he must get the traffic stopped so that my car could be turned round. (Because there had been no head-on impact its chassis was undamaged and it was still movable, though it was badly bashed on both sides and its near front wheel was askew. It was to emerge from being repaired as good as new.) He then tried to use his radio, and it didn't work. Never mind, he said, here comes a colleague, and another police car drew up – and his radio didn't work either, greatly embarrassing both of them. But when a third policeman arrived, this one on a motorbike, and his proved just as useless, it dawned on all of us that we must be in a blank spot where there was no reception. From then on, at every stage of the drama – stopping the traffic, starting it up again, summoning the AA (in vain – they deal only with breakdowns, not accidents), finding a firm in Newmarket to tow in and repair the car – the unfortunate bike man had over and over again to speed to the nearest round-about ahead, turn to speed to the nearest roundabout astern, then turn to speed back to us, all in order to make radio calls, because it seemed that they all relied on their radio equipment so trustingly that they carried no mobiles. I was there on that shoulder for over an hour and a half before a breakdown van arrived to convey me to the repair works in Newmarket.

Once there, I realized that I was feeling distinctly unwell: shock had turned into a general physical malaise. Offered a courtesy car, I accepted it because I was still fifty-odd miles from my destination, but I was not at all sure that I would be able to drive it. There was something quite unreal about standing in that quiet office where people addressed me as though I were a normal customer, while in fact I was someone who ought to be a dead body trapped in a tangle of metal probably surrounded by a number of other dead or damaged bodies in similar tangles. I felt apologetic for being so oddly unreal, although no one seemed to be noticing.

Then, suddenly, Mrs Mattocks and her first-aid classes over sixty years ago, at the beginning of the war, loomed into my mind: our district nurse, very stout (my brother and I referred to her, alas, as Mrs Buttocks), whose task it was to prepare the village for invasion. Mrs Mattocks always said that in cases of shock by far the best thing was Hot Sweet Tea . . . and what was that in the corner of the office where I was stranded? A tea-making machine, with little envelopes of sugar in a paper cup beside it. Of course they allowed me to make myself a cup of tea, into which I put four envelopes of sugar – and Mrs Mattocks had been perfectly right! Halfway through that cup, click, and I came together. By the time it was finished I felt normal. Once in my courtesy car, I drove carefully and slowly but without a qualm. And from then on that horrible accident had so little effect on my nerves that now I say to myself, 'With nerves as strong as that you can go on driving for at least another year. After all, the scars so far have been only on my car, not on people.'

11

WHEN YOU BEGIN discussing old age you come up against reluctance to depress either others or yourself, so you tend to focus on the more agreeable aspects of it: coming to terms with death, the continuing presence of young people, the discovery of new pursuits and so on. But I have to say that a considerable part of my own old time is taken up by doing things or (worse) failing to do things for people older, or if not older, less resistant to age, than myself. Because not everyone ages at the same rate, it is probable that eventually most people will either have to do some caring, or be cared for, and although the former must be preferable to the latter, I don't think I am unusual in having failed to understand in advance that even the preferable alternative is far from enjoyable. Or perhaps that is just my reaction to it. There certainly are unselfish people with a bent for caring to whom it seems to come more naturally. But I can speak only for those like myself, to whom it doesn't.

It is with Barry that this has become apparent – also, to a certain extent, with my oldest friend, Nan Taylor, who died recently, but with her I was one of a team of friends who rallied round, so although it lasted for two years or so it was never full-time. With Barry, it is, or ought to be.

He and I met in 1960, when he was still married and wishing he wasn't. This was not because he didn't love his wife, but because he had become sure of something he had always suspected and had foolishly attempted to ignore: he is temperamentally unfitted for marriage. He detests possessing and being possessed, not just in theory but with every atom of his being. Convinced that he didn't love his wife less because of liking, or even loving, other women, he was unable to feel that she was reasonable when she disagreed with him, thus forcing him to deceive her, which he disliked doing. A typical unfaithful husband, in fact, though with a stronger than usual conviction of being in the right, so sure was he that an over-riding need to be someone's One and Only is neurotic, unwholesome and the cause of many ills.

And I, at the age of forty-three (eight years older than he) felt much the same. I had turned my back with a good deal of relief on romantic love, and I had become so used to not being married that only with difficulty, and without enthusiasm, could I imagine the alternative. We came together, therefore, with no thought of marriage, simply because we liked and were physically attracted to each other, and agreed with each other about what made good writing and acting (Barry wrote plays), both of us valuing clarity and naturalness above all. We had a lot to talk about together in those days, and when he said to me that if he and his wife ever did break up, the one thing he was sure of was that he would never marry again, I remember feeling relieved: I needn't feel guilt! It was even a comfort to know that for now, anyway, there was someone else there to wash his shirts and feed him – I could enjoy all the plums of love without having to wade through the pudding. I marvelled at having gone through so much of the froth and flurry of romantic loving in my youth, when it had now become apparent that being the Other Woman suited me so very well. Our relationship gradually became firmer and firmer, more and more obviously likely to endure, but it never changed from being more like a loving friendship than an obsession.

Finally the marriage did break up (not because of me, though for reasons of convenience I agreed to being cited as the cause) and Barry set about living on his own, at which he was very bad. I can no longer remember exactly how and why he moved in to share my flat – it made little difference to the amount we were seeing of each other – but I think it was after we had stopped being lovers. Yes: piecing together scraps of memory in a way that would be tedious to go into, I am sure it was. But because there was such a gradual move from love affair into settled companionship, it is no longer possible for me to date this.

What I can date, however, is the much later beginning of Barry's illness. It was in January 2002. In fact he had begun to be diabetic some time earlier, with the less acute form of diabetes which strikes in old age, but at first he was unaware of it and then the doctor he happened to consult made light of it, telling him not to worry because it could easily be controlled by medication and a sensible diet. The only parts of that advice he heeded were 'not to worry' and 'medication'. He assured himself and me that all he need do was take his pill and forget about it, that was what Doctor X had said. Doctor X. Given what happened later, it is lucky for her, my publisher and me that I have genuinely forgotten her name. Barry had got himself onto her books before we were living together, when his health was fine, and had decided he liked her. And I, knowing nothing about diabetes except that in its acute form the patient is dependent on insulin injections so what a relief that this was not going to be necessary for Barry, was happy to let him potter along in what I didn't realize was his folly.

Why I failed to recognize his folly was because, except for one emergency which had been dealt with by his wife, I had never known him in anything but excellent health. Not so much as a cold, or a headache, or an attack of indigestion, had he ever had in my experience of him. It is true that his attitude to illness in others was simplistic: 'Is it cancer?', 'Is he going to die?', 'Is he in pain?' were his inevitable questions, and reassured on those points he would dismiss the matter. But it took me quite a while to see that when he himself had to consult a doctor all he paid attention to was the question of pain, which he was less able to tolerate than anyone else I have ever known. If he is hurting, then he becomes frantic for the doctor to stop it. 'Give me morphine!' he insists, and considers the withholding of it an outrage. This, it turned out, was because the one, wife-attended emergency, a twisted gut, had caused him agony, which was eased only when a friend from his days as an undergraduate at Cambridge, who had become a doctor, smuggled him some morphine which not only plunged him into blissful comfort, but also cured him – or so it seemed. So now, if something hurts, he will demand morphine, but any other kind of problem he can't bring himself to think about. As soon as a doctor, or nurse, or anyone else starts giving him advice about diet, or explaining any kind of treatment other than the simply analgesic, he *visibly* switches off. Something inside him decides: 'This is going to be boring, even disagreeable advice, so I shan't listen.' And that's that.

He didn't keep up the pottering for long. Early in January 2002 Doctor X sent him up to the Royal Free Hospital for some kind of minor intervention on his penis, and two days later his waterworks seized up. This process I shall not describe, for which you should be grateful. It is an excruciating business, which involved us in a midnight run by ambulance to Accident and Emergency, where we had a four-hour wait, Barry in increasing agony, before a doctor appeared to put him on a catheter . . . on which, for a complexity of reasons, he was to remain *for three months* before the simple operation on his prostate gland which would end that particular trouble (which was not cancer) was performed. It doesn't take long for anyone on a catheter to learn that the basic discomfort and humiliation is the least of it, because painful infections become frequent. We were soon miserably accustomed to those emergency ambulance runs and those grim hours in Accident and Emergency, but nothing was more appalling than when, having at last called him in for his operation, they then cancelled it at the last minute on the grounds that his heart was not up to it (grounds which luckily, but mysteriously, vanished later), and sent him home without a word as to what was to happen next. Unable to get any information from the hospital, I called Dr X in desperation, asking, 'But is he going to have to continue on a catheter for the rest of his life?' To which she replied: 'Poor Barry. It does sometimes happen, I'm afraid.'

Weeks later, we learnt that a letter from the hospital about Barry's treatment was lying unopened on her desk. What was going on there we never discovered, but from our point of view she, our only hope, was simply fading away. For some time, when I went to her surgery to collect his diabetes pills, they were forthcoming – there was even a short time when I thought what a nice surgery it was compared to my own doctor's, never any wait, without asking myself why there was hardly ever anyone there but me! Then, if one needed to see her, the answer would be: 'Doctor's not in today, perhaps if you tried tomorrow afternoon.' If you asked could you see her partner instead: 'I'm afraid he is out on a call.' And so on and so on, until the day when the answer came as an hysterical-sounding shriek: '*There is no doctor at this surgery.*' At which point I was able to persuade Barry that he would be better off under my own doctor. Not that it got him any nearer his operation.

Given three months of the National Health at its groggiest plus Dr X, both Barry and I were eventually reduced to the condition of zombies – and we were reasonably alert and well-informed old people. What it would have done to less privileged oldies, heaven knows. We ceased to believe that anything we did or said could do any good; no one was ever going to tell us anything, and if they did we would be fools to believe them; so we sank into doing nothing, just sitting there miserably waiting for who knew what. It was our beloved Sally who rescued us. It was she who came up to London, called the consultant's Harley Street number and made an appointment for Barry as a private patient. And my word, the difference £225 can make! The mysterious figure protected by a flock of white coats, vanishing round distant corners of corridors, became a pleasant and reassuring man ready to answer all our questions with lucid explanations. No no no, of course Barry was not going to remain on a catheter for ever, that hardly ever happened and he was sure it wouldn't do so in this case. The delay was simply because he was not going to operate without further consultation with the cardiac specialist so that he could decide between using a normal anaesthetic or an epidural, and the cardiac specialist happened to be away on his holiday and would not be back for another three weeks. Only when we got home after that meeting did it occur to me that this was an amazingly long holiday. Sitting face to face with the consultant our gratitude for having questions answered as though we were rational adults was so extreme that we ceased to be anything of the sort. The humiliations of illness go deep: we didn't cease to be zombies, we just became, for the moment, happy zombies.

The three weeks became nearer five, and very long weeks they were – long enough to include fretful telephone calls (when the consultant announced that he was going to operate tomorrow, he added pettishly 'I was going to operate tomorrow *anyway*, it's nothing to do with those telephone calls', which instantly made me suppose that it was). And it was successful, though the wound took several weeks to heal and a few more infections had to be fought off. But Barry has never recovered his health.

While all this was going on I did something I had never done before. I kept a diary. It was written in fat chunks with long gaps in between, not day by day, so it is more retrospective than diaries usually are, and it gives a better picture of what happened to our relationship than anything I could write now.

I can't remember whether, at the beginning of Barry and me, I felt a passing scruple at taking up so quickly and enthusiastically with yet another married man. I suppose I may have done. But I *can* remember quite clearly thinking what a *comfort* it was that he had a nice, competent wife to look after him, so I needn't ever worry on his behalf. And when, after Mary kicked him out, he ended up living with me, the 'not-having-to-take-care' didn't change much. By then we'd gone off the boil sexually and he was even less keen than I was about 'marriedness', so it was more like friends deciding to share a flat than the setting-up of a ménage. There was never, for instance, any question of my doing his washing, and he was always ready to share the cooking. In recent years, when his eccentricities began to take over to the extent of sometimes being a bit of a bore, and mine the same no doubt, all we had to do was drift gently into going even more our own ways, so it has never been claustrophobic. I think it must be quite rare for a relationship to be as enjoyable as ours was for the first eight years or so, and simultaneously so undemanding. And then for the undemandingness to continue contentedly for the next forty-odd years!

And then – this prostate trouble. Although the habit of not looking after him was ingrained – well, you *just can't* disregard the seizing up of someone's urinary system. That dreadful night when we had to dial 999 for the emergency ambulance plunged us into a situation where looking after just had to be done.

It was interesting to learn that while I was dismayed at having to spend so much time doing things for him or worrying about him, nothing in me questioned for a moment that so it must be. The dismay, though real enough, was on the surface, while something underneath and not even thought about took it for granted that what was necessary had to be done.

I was most forcibly struck by the extent of my acceptance of the situation when, during one of his spells in hospital, he became constipated, largely because the catheter he was on then was a bad one which caused him to suffer spasms at the slightest provocation. This frightened him so that he was reluctant to move – froze him up. Eventually they gave him a laxative, and when I arrived that afternoon a nurse said, 'I've been trying to get him to the toilet, but he refused to go till you came.' And as soon as I reached his bedside he said, 'Thank god you're here, now I can go to the loo.' [Here I shall spare you several lines of over-detailed description, returning to the scene near its end.] Luckily there were lots of substantial paper towels in the loo, and a large covered bin into which to dispose of them, and plenty of hot water: it was not difficult to clean him, the pan and the floor up. What astonished me was that I didn't mind doing it. There was no recoil, no feeling of disgust – I seemed to *watch myself* doing it in a businesslike way, without making any effort, like a professional nurse. But at the same time I was surprised at this. And indeed, I still feel surprised. Not so much at having done it, but at not having to make an effort to do it. (When Barry was back in bed he remarked that it was lucky that I had been there. I answered rather tartly that he could perfectly well have gone to the loo with the nurse, to which he replied, 'Yes, but it would have been less pleasant' !!!) After that, I realized that I had moved, after all those years, into a state of Wifehood. Having recognized that, and thought that after such a long time of happy exemption it was perhaps only fair that I should have a taste of munching the pudding, I stopped minding the loss of 'my own way' quite so much. But my word, what bliss any escape into it always is!

It was just as well that this automatic shift into wifehood came about, because I have had to remain in it ever since. Barry's prostate trouble was over, but his diabetes became worse, so that quite soon he had to add insulin injections to his treatment. These, to my relief, he was willing to administer himself, but they have never made him feel any better. Most diabetics seem to be able to live normal lives once their treatment has been decided on and they have learnt how to manage their diet, but Barry, perhaps because he refuses to make any effort to eat right, feels permanently exhausted and hardly ever able to leave his bed. And I – this causes pangs of guilt, but not strong enough pangs to produce much action – have found it impossible to take control of his diet with an iron hand, which would involve not only a great deal of cooking, but also compelling him to eat things he doesn't like, which no one has ever been able to do. While as for preventing him from eating what he does like . . . Naturally I avoid buying cakes, sweet biscuits and so on, whereupon this bedridden man, who has to be driven to the library three or four times a week in order to keep him in reading matter, will, as soon as I am out, get himself to the shops in order to buy a coffee cake or doughnuts without a moment's hesitation, and will stop this idiocy only when his blood-sugar readings go through the ceiling and he feels really terrible. He will then be sensible until the readings become not too bad (they are never very good), at which point he will start all over again, while to wean him from fats and from huge dollops of double cream in his coffee is simply impossible. It is some consolation to me that both Sally and her daughter Jess, who know him as well as I do, are equally unable to control him and assure me that there is nothing I can do about it, but still I can't help feeling that the sort of 'wife' I have shrunk into being is a very bad one.

Our main trouble is that what he calls his 'weakness' – the dreadful draining-away of energy from which he suffers – goes so deep that he has lost interest in almost everything. This intelligent man will now read nothing but crime fiction, and never a whole book of that. At the library he will pick at random five or six such books from the shelves, and the next day will want to take them back because (surprise surprise!) they are 'unreadable', but if you give him something else he will say he 'can't be bothered'. Neither can he be 'bothered' with anything on television except sport, and less and less of that: quite often nowadays I will go into his room while the television is on and find him lying facing away from it. He no longer ever volunteers conversation, and responds to other people's attempts with monosyllables. Days and days go by without his saying anything to me but 'What are we having for supper?' and 'Will you take me to the library?' This means that almost the only pleasure left to him is food, so that depriving him of foods he enjoys seems like cruelty, and I am unable to prevent myself feeling from time to time that if a life so severely diminished is shortened by eating doughnuts, what will it matter?*

He had a flash of return to himself in the summer of 2006, when the Royal Court did a season of readings in their Theatre Upstairs of the plays which made them famous during the 1960s, which included *Skivers*, one of his. This reading was directed by Pam Brighton, who had directed its first performance, and the Royal Court's casting director had got together a wonderful cast of young actors (most of the characters in the play are schoolboys). Although excited at the prospect of it, we had no idea what to expect, so it was a glorious surprise when it turned out to be so well done that within minutes the full house forgot that it was watching a reading and felt that it was watching an excellent full performance of the play. The audience was as responsive as any playwright could wish, and when at the end Barry had to go on stage to thank everyone concerned, and said in a choked voice (looking so small and old), 'I never, ever, expected to see that play

---

* It has turned out, since this was written, that he has serious heart trouble on top of his diabetes.

again,' they rose to him. Sally and I were crying, and Jess and Beachy, who had never seen a play of his, were ecstatic ('But it's the best play I've ever seen!' Jess kept saying), and the post-play party in the bar was a lovely hugger-mugger of old friends and happiness. But when I said in the taxi on the way home 'Do you think it may have started you up again?' he answered calmly, 'Oh no, it won't do that.' And it didn't.

Our life went back to being, in about equal parts, both sad and boring. What, I sometimes ask myself, keeps me and, I am sure, innumerable other old spouses or spouselike people in similar situations, going through the motions of care? The only answer I can produce appears in the shape of a metaphor: in a plant there is no apparent similarity between its roots and whatever flower or fruit appears at the top of its stem, but they are both part of the same thing, and it seems to me that obligations which have grown out of love, however little they resemble what they grew out of, are also part of the same thing. How, if that were not so, could they be so effortlessly binding in spite of being so unwelcome? One doesn't, in these situations, make a choice between alternatives because there doesn't seem to *be* an alternative. Perhaps a wonderfully unselfish person (and they do exist) gets satisfaction from making a good a job of it. If you are a selfish one, you manage by contriving as many escapes and compensations as you can while still staying on the job. It is not an admirable solution, but I don't suppose I am the only old person to resort to it.

12

MY ESCAPES HAVE been into gardening, drawing, pottering and – the one I use most often – into books: reading them, reviewing them or (a new use of this particular occupation) writing them. I say 'a new use', but it is new only as far as I am concerned. I have just been reading Jenny Uglow's life of Mrs Gaskell, and if ever someone perfected employment of this method, she did, having had the luck to be born with enough energy for at least ten people. The obligations she accepted willingly, even happily, and survived by dodging, were those of marriage and motherhood, and neither her husband nor her daughters ever had cause to complain; but somehow she managed to clear spaces in her intensely busy life in which to be purely herself, and write her books. Or perhaps it was less a matter of clearing spaces than of having the ability to concentrate her attention fully on what she wanted to do in whatever space, however limited, became available. It is odd that she is so often considered a rather humdrum figure, when she was in fact one of dazzling vitality, a quality much to be envied. Dwindling energy is one of the most boring things about being old. From time to time you get a day when it seems to be restored, and you can't help feeling that you are 'back to normal', but it never lasts. You just have to resign yourself to doing less – or rather, to taking more breaks than you used to in whatever you are doing. In my case I fear that what I most often do less of is my duty towards my companion rather than the indulgence of my private inclinations.

Reviewing books, which I do most often for the *Literary Review*, doesn't go far towards paying the household bills, but is enjoyable because as Rebecca West once said in a *Paris Review* interview, 'it makes you really open your mind towards the book'. It also pushes me towards books I might not otherwise read. Frederick Brown's very stout life of Flaubert, for instance: if I had seen it on one of my visits to our local bookshop (which happily shows no sign of 'struggling' to survive, as people say such businesses are now doing), I would probably have thought 'interesting – but so *fat* and I've no room left on my shelves even for thin books, and anyway I know a fair amount about Flaubert already', and veered off towards the new paperbacks, thus depriving myself of a real feast of enjoyment. And Gertrude Bell – why had I never wanted to read anything by or about her, in spite of loving Freya Stark and taking it for granted that T. E. Lawrence was worth reading even though I didn't much like him? I believe the shaming reason is simply her name. Gertrude: those two syllables, which seem to me ugly, have always evoked the image of a grimly dowdy and disagreeable woman, and I'm sure I would never have picked up Georgina

Howell's biography of Bell if the *Literary Review* hadn't asked me to review it – and there, suddenly, was that truly extraordinary woman, to be followed deep into one of the world's most fascinating regions and a hair-raising passage of recent history. It was ridiculous to have known nothing about her until now, but what a wonderful discovery to be pushed, or led, into in one's eighty-ninth year!

(If I may be forgiven a lapse into senile rambling, I'm unable to explain why that name conjured disagreeable dowdiness, because the only Gertrude I ever actually knew was my great-aunt Gertie, whose aura was one not of dowdiness but of tragedy spiced with comedy, poor woman. She was one of the four handsome daughters of Dr Bright, Master of University College, Oxford, a widower who raised his children with the help of his wife's sister and made, on the whole, a good job of picking out suitable husbands for them from among the undergraduates who passed through his care. But with Gertie . . . well, she fell in love with and was either engaged to, or on the verge of being engaged to, not an undergraduate but a junior fellow of his college. And one morning the parlour maid knocked on the door of the Master's study to announce that there was a lady downstairs, with a little boy, who was asking to see him. 'Show her up,' said the Master, and she did, and no sooner was the lady through the door than she whipped out of her muff a pistol and shot him. 'L-l-l-luckily she shot me in p-p-p-profile,' he was to tell a colleague (he had a famous stammer), so his portliness was only grazed, not punctured. The lady, it turned out, was the junior fellow's wife, or perhaps only felt she ought to be. It was a long time before this story was told in a hushed voice to the oldest of my cousins, and another long time before she passed it on to the rest of us, so its details were slightly blurred, but I have since learnt that it was a well-known incident in the college's history. Gertie recovered from what must have been a dreadful shock in time to marry a bishop, but while my grandmother and her other two sisters gave the impression of comfortable assurance, she always seemed to me to be a little frail and querulous.)

Back to books. I am puzzled by something which I believe I share with a good many other oldies: I have gone off novels. When I was young I read almost nothing else, and all through fifty years of working as a publisher fiction was my principal interest, so that nothing thrilled me more than the first work of a gifted novelist. Of course there are many novels which I remember with gratitude – and some with awe – and there are still some which I admire and enjoy; but over and over again, these days, even when I acknowledge that something is well written, or amusing, or clever, I start asking myself before I have gone very far into it, 'Do I want to go on with this?', and the answer is 'No'.

The novel has several ways of hooking a reader: offering escape into thrills and/or the exotic, offering puzzles to be solved, offering daydream material; offering a reflection of your own life; offering revelation of other kinds of life; offering an alternative to recognizable life in the shape of fantasy. It can set out to make you laugh, make you cry, make you gasp with amazement. Or, at its best, it can take you into a completely real-seeming world in which you can experience all those sensations. I well remember my feelings as I approached the end of my first reading of *Middlemarch*: 'Oh no – I'm going to have to leave this world, and I don't want to!'

I never responded with enthusiasm to thrills, puzzles or fantasies, but in my teens I gulped daydream material for quite a while before moving on to 'complete worlds', which is what I prefer to this day when I can find them. But in the 1950s and '60s I veered off towards novels that reflected, more or less, my own life. If they depended on that kind of recognition from people who were not quite like me, then I had no time for them – Angela Thirkell's books, for example, which were catnip to a kind of middle-class Englishwoman not respected by me. But Margaret Drabble's – how cross I was when Weidenfeld captured Margaret Drabble, who hit off the kind of people and situations familiar to me so exactly that I longed to publish her as well as read her. The 'NW1 novel' seemed new at the time, and for several years it was the kind I turned to most eagerly, thoroughly enjoying each moment in a love affair or other kind of relationship which was observed with special accuracy. But eventually novels of that kind seemed to develop a slow puncture, so that gradually they went flat on me; or rather, that happened to my reception of them. I became bored with what they had to tell me: I knew it too well. And because a great many of today's novels still focus mainly on the love lives of the kind of women I see around me all the time, that means that I am bored by a large proportion of available fiction.

Happily that is not true of the fiction that takes one into the lives of people completely different from oneself, V. S. Naipaul's, for example, or Philip Roth's. And it could never apply to the giants:

Tolstoy, Eliot, Dickens, Proust, Flaubert, Trollope (yes, I put him up there, I think he has been severely underestimated). They are so rare because they are a different kind of person, just as a musical genius is: they have an imaginative energy of a kind so extraordinary that it is hardly too much to describe it as uncanny. Just occasionally a present-day novelist breaks through into their territory. I would say that David Foster Wallace does in *Infinite Jest*, exhausting though he can be; that Margaret Atwood often gets a foothold there, and Pat Barker with her series of novels about the First World War; and that Hilary Mantel definitely did with *A Place of Greater Safety* (the nerve of it – to take on the French Revolution in the shoes of Robespierre, Camille Desmoulins and Danton!).

And then, of course, there are the fiction writers whose minds one falls in love with regardless of the kind of book they are writing – for me, Chekhov, W. G. Sebald and Alice Munro, but I am not going to attempt an analysis of the attraction of those three very different writers because it would take three separate chapters of a different kind of book, and anyway I am a reader not a critic, so probably couldn't do it even if I wanted to. So 'going off' novels doesn't mean that I don't think being able to write them is a wonderful and enviable gift, only that old age has made me pernickety, like someone whose appetite has dwindled so that she can only be tempted by rare delicacies. The pernicketiness does not extend to non-fiction because the attractiveness of non-fiction depends more on its subject than it does on its author's imagination.

I no longer feel the need to ponder human relationships – particularly not love affairs – but I do still want to be fed facts, to be given material which extends the region in which my mind can wander; and probably the best example of the kind of thing I am grateful for is the way my understanding of the early stages of the industrial revolution has been enlarged by three – no, four – books.

The first of them is *Pandaemonium*, that marvellous compendium of material collected over many years by Humphrey Jennings, published long after his death as a result of devoted work by his daughter Mary-Lou with the help of Charles Madge, and subtitled 'The Coming of the Machine as Seen by Contemporary Observers, 1660–1886'. Because of the astonishing variety and high quality of the texts and the way they are put together, this book generates an addictive excitement of the mind. I couldn't possibly have stopped reading it halfway through, and it left me with an acute awareness of how the delights of discovery and achievement led to tragic consequences as they became more and more orientated towards profit – how idealism capsized into greed and squalor. (We published this book in 1985, but didn't manage to sell many copies of it, so it will be hard to find nowadays. If you can get hold of a copy, I strongly advise you to do so.) The second and third books are a biography, Brian Dolan's life of Josiah Wedgwood, and letters, those of Charles Darwin. Wedgwood's life exemplifies so vividly that moment in history when men suddenly sensed that in science and technology they had found an 'open sesame' to great things . . . To great and *good* things, so Wedgwood and his friends Thomas Bentley, Joseph Priestley and Erasmus Darwin firmly believed, because enlightenment was surely going to be moral as well as intellectual. Wedgwood, within a comparatively short lifetime, turned the simple trade of potter into a dazzling industry, first by discovering the scientist in himself, then (and this is what is so moving about him) by believing that what mattered was doing things as well as you possibly could, which would inevitably lead to success, and that nothing but good could come for the working man from technological advance as a result. It is true that shortly before his death omens did begin to blur the innocence of this vision, but still it is impossible not to envy the climate of hope in which he lived. And Charles Darwin's letters, particularly those of his youth, illustrate not only his own developing genius, but the way in which the most ordinary lives – those of country doctors, clergymen, squires, tradesmen – were also being stirred by ripples of science: how everywhere people were tapping rocks, collecting shells, dissecting plants, observing birds. It was this eagerness to learn by scientific observation that provided the atmosphere in which Thomas Bewick flourished, and it is his life story, told to what I can only call perfection by Jenny Uglow, which is my fourth book.

Bewick himself did not embrace what was 'modern' in his day with much enthusiasm. He adhered to the traditional techniques of wood-engraving, he abhorred enclosure, and he much preferred the tremendously long walks he undertook as a young and middle-aged man to the train journeys which had become possible when he was old. But his innate gifts as a naturalist and his brilliance as an artist brought him fame because they answered what was then a 'modern' need, and in his private life his keen discussion of new developments in science and politics with his fellow tradesmen – the creativity and intellectual liveliness that blossomed among these men of little education, who often gathered together in clubs or debating societies such as Newcastle's 'Lit.and Phil.', the Literary and Philosophical Society to which Bewick belonged and which is still in existence – was typical of this fecund time. It is evoked with such sensitivity, and in such rich detail, by Uglow as she brings to life the passionate, vulnerable, eccentric, reliable, wholly lovable man she clearly hates to leave behind at the end of her book.

I have gained much from many non-fiction books, but will let those four stand for them all. What refreshment, to be able to take a holiday from oneself in such good company.

Another kind of reading which is common among old people, and which I indulge in quite often, is returning to old favourites. Often this is pure pleasure, but sometimes it makes me see that even the run-of-the-mill novel of today is much more sophisticated and interesting than that of my early youth, not to mention those popular just before the First World War, books bought by my parents when they were young which were still on our shelves when I began to move on from children's books, so that I read them too, and enjoyed them. Everyone in my family was familiar with, and loved, the classics, but naturally what they mostly read was the equivalent of what is reviewed on the literary pages of today, ranging from the seriously good to the cosy Aga-saga or Bridget Jones type of entertainment, and some of these still lurk in the little Norfolk house where I spend many weekends. From time to time I pull one out, just to remind myself, and end up unsure whether I am more dismayed or amused. The best of them seem ponderous and verbose, over-given to description (what a lot about cutting from here to there we have learnt from the cinema!), while as for the rest! Infantile tosh: that is what they so often are.

At the end of the 1800s and during the pre-war years of the twentieth century there was an extraordinary fashion for 'historical' romances. A few of them, books by Dumas and Rider Haggard, for example, are saved by imaginative vigour and a gift for story-telling – though perhaps I like Haggard just because he was 'ours', the Haggards being neighbours of my grandparents, so that we went to parties with his grandchildren and on most Sundays listened to Sir Rider reading the lessons in church (very dramatically – his rendering of Shadrach, Meshach and Abednego in the burning fiery furnace was long remembered). But there was a teeming undergrowth of books such as those of Jeffery Farnol, who favoured chapter headings like 'How and Why I Fought With One Gabbing Dick, a Pedlar' or 'In Which I Begin to Appreciate the Virtues of the Chaste Goddess', or Agnes and Egerton Castle, of whose *If Youth But Knew* the following is a typical paragraph:

'What things,' said the fiddler, addressing his violin as the court fool of old his bauble (after the singular fashion which led people to call him crazy) – 'what things, beloved, could we not converse upon tonight, were we not constrained by sinners? What a song of the call of the spring to last year's fawn – of the dream which comes to the dreamer but once in his life's day, and that before the dawn? Chaste and still as the night, and yet tremulous; shadows, mere shadows, yet afire; voiceless, formless, impalpable, yet something more lovely than all the sunshine can show, than all the beauty arms can hold hereafter, than all the music ears shall hear . . . O youth! O love!' sighed the fiddler, and drew from his fiddle a long echo to the sigh.

In these novels young women were called maidens and were wilful but chaste, sometimes defiant, but if so, absolutely certain to end by yielding tremulously to a young man who may have been wrong-headed to start with but proved stunningly honourable when it came to the crunch, and this pair was more than likely to encounter a picturesque tinker or itinerant musician, or suchlike, possessed of endless funds of wry wisdom. Heroes and heroines were of noble, or at least extremely gentle, birth, although because their breeding was *true* they would mingle happily with peasants or with those tinkers (a fairly frequent device was to have them disguised as humbler beings, thus allowing for misunderstandings and revelations). The reverence for class in these books was blatant. The novel in Britain is still a middle-class phenomenon, but no longer so fatuously as it was then. And these ridiculous books were cheerfully enjoyed by intelligent adults – and by me, in my early teens. So who knows what will be made a hundred years or so from now of the perfectly acceptable fiction of which I, and many other old people, have had enough? Perhaps we shall be proved right.

I depend so much on reading because I never developed the habit of watching television. I have never even bought a set. In 1968 I was given one by the woman who used to clean for me, because it had started to go into snaky waves at crucial moments and she was replacing it with one less tiresome, and for a few weeks I watched it all of every evening, always hoping that the next thing to appear on the screen would be wonderful, and it wasn't. So then I put it in my lodger's room, and in that room, now Barry's, it still is (or rather, its successor is – he has replaced it several times), watched by me only for Wimbledon and the Derby, or when Tiger Woods is playing. I used to watch the Grand National too, but can no longer bear to do so because of horses being killed. (Though quite tough when young, now I find any sort of cruelty unwatchable and, if vivid, unreadable: I couldn't read all of even my much admired William Dalrymple's *The Last Mughal*, which describes the destruction of Delhi in 1857, a brilliant and important book, because of the horrors he was having to report. The routine horrors in the daily news are different, in that one *has* to be aware of those, though I dwell on details as little as possible.) I am always embarrassingly at a loss when people discuss television programmes, as they so often do, and the many columns of newsprint devoted to television are meaningless babble to me, but although I realize this ignorance is truly nothing to be proud of, I have to suppose that some foolish part of my mind is attached to it, because I have never been able to remedy it. It is easier to imagine returning to radio than buying a television set. I once listened to Radio Three a lot, being hungry for music, but now that deafness has distorted most musical sounds to the point of ugliness, I have given that up. If, however, I become unable to read, which god forbid, I expect Radio Four will become welcome. I have dear friends in New York who are almost ready to move to London for the sake of Radio Four.

13

THE ACTIVITIES I escape into are mostly ordinary things which have become more valuable because I am old, enjoyed with increasing intensity because of the knowledge that I shan't be able to enjoy them for much longer; but easily the best part of my old age has been, and still is, a little less ordinary. It is entirely to do with having had the luck to discover that I can write. I don't suppose that I shall carry it as far as my friend Rose Hacker, who at the age of a hundred is the oldest newspaper columnist in Britain (she writes for the *Camden News*), but it looks as though it will still be with me when (if!) I reach my ninetieth birthday, and it is impossible adequately to describe how grateful I am for that.

It took me by surprise, and has done so twice, which appears to be unusual, because the majority of writers seem to know quite early in their lives that writing is what they want to do. I knew from early childhood that I loved books, and from my early teens that I enjoyed writing letters and was considered by my friends to write good ones, but I didn't aspire to writing books, probably because when I was young 'books' meant 'novels', and I lack the kind of imagination a novelist must have: the ability to create characters and events and even (in cases of genius) whole worlds. And probably the fact that my love of other people's writing led me into a career as an editor meant that much of whatever creative energy I possessed found an outlet in my daily work, so that it took many years to build up perceptible pressure.

But pressure did build, making its first appearance in the form of little outbreaks like those small hot springs that bubble up here and there in volcanic territory: nine short stories, none of them planned. There would be an agreeable sort of itchy feeling, a first sentence would appear from nowhere, and blip, out would come a story. One of them won the *Observer*'s short-story competition, an intoxicating thrill in that it showed I had been putting down words in the right way, but it didn't make any more stories come after a tenth had fizzled out after two pages. That was followed by a lull of almost a year. Then, looking for something in a rarely opened drawer, I happened on those two pages, and read them. Perhaps, I thought, something could be made of them after all, so the next day I put paper in my typewriter and this time it wasn't blip, it was whoosh! – and *Instead of a Letter*, my first book, began. Those stories had been no more than hints of what was accumulating in the unconscious part of my mind, and the purpose of that accumulation, which I hadn't known I needed, was healing.

Twenty years earlier I'd had my heart broken, after which I had gradually learnt to live quite comfortably by accepting – so I thought – that as a woman I was a failure. Now, when this book turned out to be an account of that event which was as nearly accurate as I could make it, I was cured. It was an extraordinary experience. The actual writing was extraordinary because, although I was longing all day to get back from the office and sit down to it, I never knew (and this is literally true) what the next paragraph I was going to write would be. I would quickly read the last two or three pages from the day before, and on it would instantly go; and yet, in spite of this absolute lack of method, the finished book appeared to be a carefully structured work. (It struck me then, and I am sure this is true, that a great deal of that sort of work must go on in one's sleep.) And the final result was extraordinary too, in that once the book was done the sense of failure had vanished for good and I was happier than I had ever been in my life. I was also sure that writing was what I liked doing best, and hoped that more of it would come to me.

More did come, twice in the shape of traumatic events – one the suicide of a man I had been trying to help, the other the murder of a young woman. I plunged straight into 'writing them out', as what seemed to me the natural and certain way of ridding my mind of distress, and in both cases the events in themselves made 'stories', so the experience of writing them was a good deal less mysterious than that of writing *Instead of a Letter*. 'Enjoyable' seems the wrong word for the writing of them, but absorbing – indeed consuming – it was. And of course both books 'got me over' something painful: so much so that as soon as they were finished I put them away, and away they would have stayed had friends not urged me to get them published (the second of them was in a drawer for sixteen years).

Neither of those books meant a great deal to me after they had served their purpose, though naturally I was very pleased if people spoke well of them, and the same was true of the novel which I wrote in the 1960s because my publisher nagged me. (One can't help being very pleased if told convincingly that one writes well: it's like a shot of essential vitamins to one's self-esteem). In those days anyone who wrote anything at all good that was not a novel was constantly badgered with 'And now when are you going to give us your novel?' (I never did this myself when I was a publisher because I couldn't see any sense in it. There were plenty of people around who were damn well going to give us their novel come hell or high water, anyway.) I capitulated, against my better judgement, and although I was proud of it in the end because it turned out quite a neat little book, and I still take pleasure in remembering writing parts of it, as a whole it was such appallingly hard work that I swore *never again*. What it proved was that while anyone who can write at all can squeeze out one novel at a pinch, this particular person was right in knowing herself not to be a novelist. I felt detached from that book because I had not really wanted to write it. The other two – perhaps I followed their fortunes with less interest than those of *Instead of a Letter* simply because I had become slightly embarrassed at making public things usually considered private, and for a private reason. I believed, and still believe, that there is no point in describing experience unless one tries to get it as near to being what it really was as you can make it, but that belief does come into conflict with a central teaching in my upbringing: Do Not Think Yourself Important.

Much as I wanted to continue to write, I found it impossible unless something was itching to come out. I could cover paper easily in ordinary ways such as letters, blurbs, reviews of books and so on, but if I tried to tell a story or examine a subject because that was what, intellectually, I wanted to do, not because there was pressure inside me to do it, the writing would be inert. With persistence, I could go on covering paper, but plod plod plod it would go until I was bored out of my mind. It is hard to explain, probably because I have never been able to force myself to examine it, but it seems to be something to do with hitting on a rhythm – perhaps getting down to a level at which that rhythm exists. Without it, my sentences are dead. With it, and I can always tell when I have hit it, don't ask me how, the sentences start to flow as though on their own. Real writers, I am sure, are more disciplined than this and must be able to keep themselves at it, as well as being, no doubt, gifted with readier access to that mysterious rhythm. My own dependence on a specific kind of stimulus has always seemed to me proof that I am an amateur – though that is not to take back the statement that 'writing is what I like doing best'.

Anyway, by the time I retired from my job, at the age of seventy-five, I hadn't written anything for a long time because it was a long time since anything had happened to me that needed curing. I was sorry about that, because I did so greatly enjoy the act of writing, but it had become so firmly attached in my mind to the *need* to write for therapeutic reasons that I couldn't envisage myself doing it for any other reason. People started saying to me 'You had fifty years in publishing, you worked with all those interesting people – you ought to write about it, you know, you really ought!' and a cloud of boredom would descend on me, out of which I would answer: 'But I don't work like that.' And that was true for at least the first two years of my retirement.

Then I began to catch myself remembering incidents from, or aspects of, the past with enough pleasure to want to dwell on them, so every now and then I would scribble a few pages about whatever it was that had floated to the surface in that way. Mostly it was about our firm's early days, because starting up a firm with almost no money and no experience at all really was great fun. (I am speaking for myself when I say 'no experience at all': André Deutsch, the moving spirit of the adventure, had only about a year's experience but had sucked out of that year more than many people gain from a lifetime.) Looking back at it I could see what an unusual and interesting time it had been and how lucky I was to have been involved in it. Once my memories reached the point at which we moved into our offices in Great Russell Street and were able confidently to consider ourselves proper publishers, the fizz went out of them. Indeed, at the thought that there were *still thirty years ahead* the cloud of boredom would reappear, because how on earth could I plod my way through thirty years without sending everyone else to sleep as well as myself? So I would push aside whatever I had just written and forget about it, until another odd or amusing memory floated up.

The two 'bits' that had become the most solid during the writing were two portraits, one of V. S. Naipaul, the other of Jean Rhys. Those I had enjoyed very much, because it pleased me to discover that I could be intensely involved in a piece of writing that had absolutely nothing to do with my own emotional development. There were, of course, feelings involved, but not at any deep level – nothing demanding 'cure'! – and to be enjoying writing simply because I was interested in the subject was a new experience. It was the Jean Rhys piece that steered the whole thing bookwards.

Jean Rhys is a writer who either irritates readers a great deal, or fascinates them. No one questions that her actual writing – the way she uses words – is wonderful, but some people can't be bothered with her ruthlessly incompetent heroines, or rather 'heroine' in the singular because the 'Jean Rhys woman' is always the same. Others find this woman profoundly touching, and guessing that she is in fact Jean Rhys herself, those of them who learn that I knew Jean well during the last fifteen years of her life always want to question me about her. Xandra Bingley, my neighbour across the street (a writer almost as good as Jean and a person so unlike her that they might belong to different species) has a friend, Lucretia Stewart, who is a fan of Jean's, and Lucretia asked Xandra to help her meet me, so Xandra asked us to lunch together. In the course of this lunch I told them that I had recently written quite a long piece about Jean, and Lucretia suggested that I send it to Ian Jack, editor of *Granta*, with which magazine she had a connection.

I knew *Granta*, of course, but I had forgotten that Ian had taken over as its editor from the American Bill Buford; and during Buford's reign, although I had admired it I had found it slightly forbidding, the natural habitat of writers like Martin Amis, for example, whose world seemed so unlike my own that I felt myself going 'square' whenever I glimpsed it. Ian was less alarming. It was not that I thought he, too, was 'square', but I did think he probably took a broader view of writing than Buford did. I had always liked his own writing and I knew that he had liked *Instead of a Letter*. Supposing I submitted something to Ian and he turned it down, I would feel that there was a sensible reason for his doing so, not just that he thought me a boring old trout: I would be disappointed, not hurt. For this rather wimpish reason, I decided to follow Lucretia's advice.

He did turn it down, explaining that it was not right for the magazine, and I had been right in thinking that it would not be a painful moment. Instead, it was an interesting one, because he added that if this piece turned out to be part of a book, then he would like to see the book. Another thing I had forgotten was that *Granta* the magazine was part of an organization which also published Granta Books. So now there was a publisher who had actually expressed an interest in a book about my life in publishing, supposing that those bits and pieces I had been playing with could be persuaded into such a form . . . They suddenly took on a new appearance in my eyes. They became worth fishing out of a drawer and being looked at seriously.

Having done that, I saw to my surprise that not a great deal more work was necessary to convert the material into a two-part book, the first part being about the building of our firm, the second part about some of the writers we published. It was not necessary to plod through all the years of the firm's existence, and it would really be about being an editor rather than a publisher, because an editor was what I had always chiefly been. It would be short, but that wouldn't matter, because to my mind erring on the side of brevity is always preferable to its opposite. The arranging, polishing and filling out (which included following an excellent suggestion of Ian's as to how it should end) turned out to be thoroughly enjoyable, so that I felt sorry when it was finished – or would have done if I had not been so pleased at having a last-minute inspiration about its title. Titles can be a headache if they don't come naturally – the hours I've spent with authors in the past, going through lists of suggestions and getting gloomier and gloomier! So this time, coming up effortlessly with the *mot juste* was most satisfying: *Stet*, that was it, hurrah! And what was more, I had brought this thing off although I was eighty.

And it *was* more, too: very much so. It may even have been the best part of the whole experience. To finish writing a book, to have it accepted at once by a publisher you respect and to see it being well-received: that, at any time of one's life, is gratifying, and to repeat the process within the next two years (as I did with *Yesterday Morning*) is even more so. But to do it when one is old . . . there are, I think, three reasons why being old makes it not just gratifying, but also *absolutely delicious*.

The first is the unexpectedness. If anyone had told me when I was in my early seventies that I was going to write another book I would have thought them mad: the odd bit of scribble for my own amusement, yes – perhaps. But never a book, because there was no book there to be written. How could there be, when I was so long past the stage when the kind of thing which caused me to write could possibly happen to me? To which I would probably have added 'Thank god!', given how painful those things had been to live through. And then, when in fact it had turned out that I was capable of covering a sufficient number of pages simply because I was enjoying remembering first my time in publishing, then my childhood, there naturally came the thought 'This stuff is interesting to me, but why should it interest anyone else?' I could see that the publishing material might amuse people in the book trade, but they are only a tiny part of the reading public, so if I myself were a publisher to whom someone submitted *Stet*, would I risk it? Probably not. And *Yesterday Morning*? All so long ago, so out of fashion! It would not have surprised me in the least if either the publisher or the public had said 'No' to either of those books.

So it was truly amazing when both said 'Yes'. What it felt like was an unexpected and tremendous TREAT.

That was the first gain from being old. The second was that none of it mattered at the deepest level, so that all of it could be taken lightly. When you are young a great deal of what you are is created by how you are seen by others, and this often continues to be true even into middle age. It is most obvious in the realm of sex. I remember a school-fellow of mine, a plump, rather plain girl, pleasant but boring, whom I ran into by chance on a station platform about a year after our schooldays ended and failed, for a moment, to recognize because she had become beautiful. What had happened was that a dashing man known to both of us had fallen in love with her and asked her to marry him: he had seen her as lovely, so lovely in her happiness she now was, and an assured and attractive woman she was to remain. Such transformations can occur in connection with many other aspects of self-esteem, with results either benign or damaging, and there were a good many years in the early part of my grown-up life when my self-esteem was diminished by this fact. But once you are old you are beyond all that, unless you are very unlucky. Being seen as someone who had written and published a book when I was in my forties changed me (for the better, as it happened, but it could have gone the other way and been for the worse). In my eighties that couldn't happen, no event could be crucial to my self-esteem in quite that way any more, and that was strangely liberating. It meant some sort of loss, I suppose, such as the end of thrilling possibilities; but it allowed experiences to be enjoyable in an uncomplicated way – to be simply *fun*. At no other time in my life did I enjoy myself so comfortably, for so long, as I did around the time of *Stet*'s publication, and the pleasure would have been as great in connection with *Yesterday Morning* if its publication hadn't coincided with the worry of Barry's operation.

The third gain was related to the second: I no longer suffered from shyness. In the past my job had occasionally involved me in having to address an audience, and I was always so afraid of drying up that I typed the whole thing out and read from it. Once I had to go to Blackpool to talk about cookery books in a vast and glittery hotel full of vast and glittery ladies who, it transpired, were the wives of men who made cutlery and were having a convention. My offering was to be made in one of the smaller, darker 'function rooms' which smelt strongly and not unsuitably of gravy, and not a single person turned up for it. The relief was great, but was oddly mingled with shame so that I couldn't fully enjoy it, particularly not when, on creeping away to my room, I found that I had forgotten to pack a book to read in bed.

Because it had always been something of an ordeal I felt nervous about my first exposure by Granta at a literary festival, not understanding how lucky I was in its being at Hay, which is the warmest and most welcoming of all such shindigs. I couldn't write anything in advance because I was to be part of a trio, three people who had written memoirs discussing their reasons for doing so, and that added to the nervousness. But one of my fellow performers was Andrea Ashworth, whose *Once in a House on Fire* I had admired so much that I had written her a fan letter, which had crossed with a fan letter she had written me about *Stet*, a comically gratifying coincidence which made our meeting at the hotel where we were both staying a happy event. Being embraced by this dazzling young woman and bumbling into our tent with her on a wave of amusing and intimate talk, changed the nature of the whole experience, so that when I looked out over that crowded audience it didn't seem surprising that they were all beaming in an apparent expectation of a good time, and I found myself actually *wanting* to communicate with them. Indeed, that evening a closet exhibitionist was released: I could make them laugh! I loved making them laugh! It was all I could do to prevent myself from trying to hog more than my allotted time for talking. And from then on standing up in front of an audience has been enjoyable, while being on *Desert Island Discs* (*much* more impressive to relations, friends and indeed many strangers than any good review had ever been) was an orgy of pleasure. And of admiration, too, because gossiping away with Sue Lawley had seemed so completely natural and spontaneous that I expected to find it considerably cut and modified when it was actually broadcast, and was astonished that not a syllable had been changed: what a pro she was, establishing such an easy atmosphere while remaining in such tight control of timing.

It is not hard to see that writers who have often been through the process of promoting their books come to find it a tedious chore, but to me, for whom it was part treat, part joke and completely unexpected, it turned out to be an agreeable part of an experience which has made my life as a whole a good deal more pleasing to contemplate. I had seen it for so long as a life of failure, but now, when I look back – who would believe it, it was nothing of the sort!

14

I T SEEMS TO me that anyone looking back over eighty-nine years *ought* to see a landscape pockmarked with regrets. One knows so well, after all, one's own lacks and lazinesses, omissions, oversights, the innumerable ways in which one falls short of one's own ideals, to say nothing of standards set by other and better people. All this must have thrown up – indeed it certainly did throw up – a large number of regrettable events, yet they have vanished from my sight. Regrets? I say to myself. What regrets? This invisibility may be partly the result of a preponderance of common sense over imagination: regrets are useless, so forget them. But it does suggest that if a person is consistently lucky beyond her expectations she ends by becoming smug. A disagreeable thought, which I suppose I ought to investigate.

The absence of regret that surprises me most is connected with childlessness, because I know that for a short time I passionately wanted a child, and then lost one. Such a loss I would expect to weigh heavily on a woman, but it never has on me. The explanation seems to be that in spite of that one incident, I have uncommonly little maternal instinct, a deficiency I think I was born with. As a child I was not just indifferent to dolls, I despised them. My very first toy, the one which had eventually to be smuggled out of my cot because of how dirty it became, was a white rabbit, and later I was fond of an elephant, but representations of children – never. And I can remember being left alone for a few minutes with a month-old baby when I was nineteen, leaning over it and studying it earnestly in an attempt to feel moved by it, and coming to the conclusion that this unattractive little creature meant nothing to me – I'd rather pick up a puppy, any day. This reaction worried me, but not deeply, because I told myself at once that when I had a child of my own I would love it. That, obviously, was how it worked, because look how inevitably women did love their own children – the instinct must come with the birth. I went on reassuring myself in that way, particularly when Paul talked happily about the children we were going to have, which he enjoyed doing: choosing names for them and so on, games I would never have played if left to myself, though I disguised that. Never once in my twenties and thirties did I hope for a child, or feel more than a vague good-will towards anyone else's child. When other women yearned towards babies I kept silent to hide my own feelings, and as for toddlers, I didn't go so far as to blame them for being what they were, but I did feel that they were tedious to have around except in very small doses.

Nevertheless I was probably right in supposing that I would love a child if I ever had one. This became apparent when I was forty-three, when my body took over from my mind and pushed me into pregnancy. It had happened before, whereupon I had terminated the pregnancy without hesitation or subsequent unhappiness, but this time something buried deep inside me woke up and decided to say: 'If you don't have a child now you never will so I'm going to get you one like it or not.' Only after I realized what had happened did it occur to me that my feckless carelessness about contraceptive measures must have been, at an unconscious level, deliberate, and even then I took it for granted that I was dismayed and must set about arranging for a termination. But when I caught myself making excuse after excuse not to take the necessary steps *just yet*, I hit on the truth: I wasn't going to take them at all; and at that point I suddenly became happy with a happiness so astonishingly complete that I still remember it with gratitude: my life would have been the poorer if I hadn't tasted it, and any child to emerge from that experience could only have been loved.

But it didn't emerge, or rather it did so in the form of a miscarriage early in the fourth of what were the happiest months of my life, during all of which I had felt dazzlingly healthy. That miscarriage very nearly killed me. I was rushed to hospital only just in time. I knew how near death I was because although by then consciousness had shrunk to within the limits of the stretcher on which I was lying in a pool of blood, I could still hear the voices of those leaning over that stretcher. They had just sent someone to fetch more blood for the transfusion they were administering, and a man said, 'Call them and tell them *to tell him to run*,' and then, to someone else, 'She's very near collapse.' Not only could I hear, but I could understand. I even thought, 'What a bloody silly euphemism,' because what was the state I was in already if it wasn't collapse? He meant death. So oughtn't I to try to think some sensible Last Thought? I made a dim attempt at it but the effort was beyond me; the best I could do was, 'Oh well, if I die I die.'

The man who had to run ran fast enough, they got me down to the theatre, they performed the curettage, and the next thing I was aware of was hands manipulating my body from stretcher to bed. For a moment I was unsure whether this was after the operation or before it, then I began to vomit from the chloroform, and simultaneously became aware that in my belly peace had been restored: I was no longer bleeding. And as though it came from down there, a great wave of the most perfect joy welled up and swept through me: I AM STILL ALIVE! It filled the whole of me, nothing else mattered. It was the most intense sensation I have ever experienced.

It swept away grief at the loss of the child. Of course I went on to feel unhappy, but it was a subdued and dreary little unhappiness, quite out of proportion with the happiness of the pregnancy. I had only one dream as a result of it, and that was a subdued and dreary little dream: I was getting off an underground train, and as the doors slid shut suddenly realized to my horror that I'd left a child on the train – running anxiously along the platform – how was I going to get to the next station before the train did, so that I could recover her (in the dream it was a little girl, though I had always thought of the child as a boy)? The feeling was one of painful anxiety rather than of loss. And after that life went back gradually, but not very slowly, to being what it had been before.

It seems very odd that what had unquestionably been an important development in my life – tremendously important – should have been diminished, almost cancelled, in that way. I think the whole thing was chemical: the body responding to the approach of menopause by pumping out more of something or other which I don't usually have much of, and after the shock ceasing to pump so that my normal condition was re-established. I don't think not feeling the loss means that I would have been a bad mother. Without the shock, if that child had been born, I would probably have been a perfectly adequate one very much like my own, who loved her children once they had reached a reasonable age better than she did when they were very young (she had nannies to bear the brunt of our infancy, so had no problem seeming to us to be all that she should be, but she was never able to disguise the slight impatience she felt with very young un-nannied grandchildren). But I can't, however hard I try, *mind* having lost the chance to prove it. Now, in my old age, I am much more interested in babies and little children than I used to be: actually delighted by them, so that the recent arrival of a baby in our house is an event which gives me great pleasure, although I'm glad that I don't have to *do* anything about that child beyond observing his progress with interest and admiration. But asking myself 'Are you really not sorry that you have no children or grandchildren of your own?' I get the answer 'Yes, really.' It is precisely because I don't and *can't* have the hassle of close involvement with the infants I encounter nowadays that I have become free to understand their loveliness and promise.

Selfishness: not, I hope, a selfishness that involves all of me, but a stubborn nub of selfishness somewhere in the middle which made me wary of anything to which one has to give one's whole self, as a mother has to give herself to an infant and a toddler. It was that which prevented me from wanting a child for so long, and then made it so easy to get over losing one. So I do have at least one major regret after all: not my childlessness, but that central selfishness in me, so clearly betrayed by the fact childlessness is not what I regret. And now I remember how my inadequacy regarding small children (I always loved them quite easily when they grew older) caused me to let down my cousin Barbara, whose house I live in, in spite of thinking her then as I think of her now as my best friend, when some forty-odd years ago she started a family. No sooner had she got three children than she and her husband separated, so that she had to raise them single-handed, working at a very demanding full-time job in order to keep them. How she struggled through those years I don't know, and I think she herself marvels at it in retrospect. But at the time what did I do to help her? Nothing. I shut my eyes to her problems, even saw very little of her, feeling sadly that she had disappeared into this tiresome world of small children – or world of tiresome small children – and she has said since then that she never dreamt of asking me for help, so aware was she of my coldness towards her brood. About that it is not just regret that I feel. It is shame.

One regret brings up another, though it is, thank goodness, less shameful. It's at never having had the guts to escape the narrowness of my life. I have a niece, a beautiful woman who I shall not name because she wouldn't like it, who is the mother of three sons, the youngest of whom will soon be following his brothers to university, and who has continued throughout her marriage to work as a restorer of paintings. Not long ago she sat at dinner beside a surgeon, and happened to say to him that if she had her time over again she would choose to train in some branch of medicine. He asked her how old she was. Forty-nine, she told him. Well, he said, she still had time to train as a midwife if she wanted to, they accepted trainees up to the age of fifty; whereupon she went home and signed up. The last time I saw her she could proudly report that she had now been in charge of six births all on her own. There had been moments, she said, when she felt 'What on earth am I doing here?', but she still couldn't imagine anything more thrilling than being present at – helping at – the beginning of new life. The most moving thing of all, she said, was when the father cried (there had been fathers present at all six births). When that happened she had to go out of the room to hide the fact that she was crying too. She is a person of the most delicate reserve, so watching her face light up when she spoke about being present at a birth filled me with envy. Having had the courage and initiative suddenly to step out of a familiar and exceptionally agreeable life into something quite different, she has clearly gained something of inestimable value. And I have never done anything similar.

It is not as though I was never impatient at having only one life at my disposal. A great deal of my reading has been done for the pleasure of feeling my way into other lives, and quite a number of my love affairs were undertaken for the same reason (I remember once comparing a sexual relationship with going out in a glass-bottomed boat). But to turn such idle fancies into action demands courage and energy, and those I lacked. Even if I had been able to summon up such qualities, I am sure I would never have moved over into anything as useful as midwifery, but think of the places to which I might have travelled, the languages I might have learnt! Greek, for example: I have quite often thought of how much I would like to speak modern Greek so that I could spend time earning a living there and getting to know the country in a serious way, but I never so much as took an evening class in it. And when I went to Oxford, I indolently chose to read English literature, which I knew I was going to read anyway, for pleasure, instead of widening my range by embarking on a scientific subject, such as biology. And never at any time did I seriously try to use my hands (except at embroidery, which I am good at). Think how useful and probably enjoyable it would be to build a bookcase! I really am sorry about that.

So there are two major regrets, after all: that nub of coldness at the centre, and laziness (I think laziness played a greater part than cowardice in my lack of initiative, though some cowardice there was). They are real, but I can't claim that they torment me, or even that I shall often think about them. And at those two I shall stop, because to turn up something even worse would be a great bore. I am not sure that digging out past guilts is a useful occupation for the very old, given that one can do so little about them. I have reached a stage at which one hopes to be forgiven for concentrating on how to get through the present.

15

HOW SUCCESSFULLY ONE manages to get through the present depends a good deal more on luck than it does on one's own efforts. If one has no money, ill health, a mind never sharpened by an interesting education or absorbing work, a childhood warped by cruel or inept parents, a sex life that betrayed one into disastrous relationships . . . If one has any one, or some, or all of those disadvantages, or any one, or some, or all of others that I can't bear to envisage, then whatever is said about old age by a luckier person such as I am is likely to be meaningless, or even offensive. I can speak only for, and to, the lucky. But there are more of them than one at first supposes, because the kind of fortune one enjoys, or suffers, does not come *only* from outside oneself. Of course much of it can be inflicted or bestowed on one by others, or by things such as a virus, or climate, or war, or economic recession; but much of it is built into one genetically, and the greatest good luck of all is built-in resilience.

By chance, just as I was beginning to consider this matter, I read in the *Guardian* an interview conducted by Alan Rusbridger with Alice Herz-Sommer, who is 103 years old, and who provides an amazing example of the importance of that quality.

Born in Prague to Jewish parents who were not religious and who knew Mahler and Kafka, she grew up to be a brilliant pianist who studied with a pupil of Liszt's, and married another very gifted musician. When Hitler invaded Czechoslovakia in 1939 she was living a happy, busy, creative life, which was of course instantly crushed. With her husband and son she was sent to Theresienstadt, the 'show case' camp in which more people survived than in other camps because the Nazis used it to prove their 'humanity' to Red Cross inspectors, although many did die there, and many many thousands more, including Alice's husband, were dispatched from there to die elsewhere. When she and her son got back home after the war she found it wasn't home any more: all of her husband's family, most of her own, and all her friends had disappeared. She moved to Israel, where she brought up her son, who became a cellist, and it was at his instigation that she came to England twenty years ago. In 2001 she had to endure his sudden death at the age of sixty-five. She now lives alone in a one-room flat in north London, and might well be expected to be a grimly forlorn old woman.

Instead, the interview was illustrated with three photographs of Alice: a radiant bride in 1931, a radiant young mother just before the war – and a radiant old woman of 103 today. The joyful expression has hardly changed. And when it comes to words, she remembers that the only person who was kind on the day they were taken to the camp was a Nazi neighbour, how thrilled she was by the freedom in Israel, how much she loves England and English people. Even more important to her is how much she still loves playing the piano for three hours every day ('Work is the best invention . . . it makes you happy to do something.' Just as strikingly as Marie-Louise Motesiczky she illustrates the luck of being born creative). And she is enchanted by the beauty of life. It is not religion that inspires her. 'It begins with this: that we are born half-good and half-bad – everybody, *everybody*. And there are situations where the good comes out and situations where the bad comes out. This is the reason why people invented religion, I believe.' So she respects the hope invested in religion although she herself has felt no need for its support. She is carried along by her extraordinary good luck in being born with a nature so firmly tilted towards optimism that in spite of all that she has endured she can still say: 'Life is beautiful, extremely beautiful. And when you are old you appreciate it more. When you are older you think, you remember, you care and you appreciate. You are thankful for everything. For everything.' She also says: 'I know about the bad, but I look only for the good.'

Although others must be awestruck by her courage, I doubt whether Alice Herz-Sommer herself would claim this positive attitude as a virtue. She compares it with that of her sister, a born pessimist – and 'born' is the key word. They were given their dispositions in the same way that one is given the colour of one's hair. But while a painful sensitivity to evil may be useful during a person's active years, providing as it sometimes does energy for the necessary, if endless, struggle against mankind's 'bad half', in old age, when one's chief concern must be how to get oneself through time with the minimum discomfort to self and inconvenience to others, it can only be a burden. Unfortunately examples such as Alice's of how an active mind and a positive outlook are what one needs in old age are not likely to be useful as 'lessons', because those able to draw on such qualities will be doing so already, and those who can't, can't. Perhaps there are some of us in between those extremes who can be inspired by her to put up a better show than we would otherwise have done.

16

ONE DOESN'T NECESSARILY have to end a book about being old with a whimper, but it is impossible to end it with a bang. There are no lessons to be learnt, no discoveries to be made, no solutions to offer. I find myself left with nothing but a few random thoughts. One of them is that from up here I can look back and see that although a human life is less than the blink of an eyelid in terms of the universe, within its own framework it is amazingly capacious so that it can contain many opposites. One life can contain serenity and tumult, heartbreak and happiness, coldness and warmth, grabbing and giving – and also more particular opposites such as a neurotic conviction that one is a flop and a consciousness of success amounting to smugness. Misfortune can mean, of course, that these swings go from better to bad and stay there, so that an individual's happy security ends in wreckage; but most lives are a matter of ups and downs rather than of a conclusive plunge into an extreme, whether fortunate or unfortunate, and quite a lot of them seem to come to rest not far from where they started, as though the starting point provided a norm, always there to be returned to. Alice's life swung in arcs far more extreme that most, but still I feel it may have followed this pattern. I suppose I think it because I have seen other lives do that, and I know that my own has done so.

Not long ago a friend said to me that I ought to be careful not to sound complacent, 'because' he added kindly, 'you are not.' I believe he was wrong there, and that I am, because complacent (not to say smug) I certainly started out during a happy childhood wrapped warmly in my family's belief that we were the best kind of people possible short of saintliness: a belief common in the upper levels of the English middle class and confirmed by pride in being English, which I remember deriving from an early introduction to a map of the world. All those pink bits were *ours*! How lucky I was not to have been born French, for example, with their miserable little patches of mauve.

This tribal smugness was not, of course, a licence to rampage. Like all such groups, ours had its regulations which one had to observe in order to earn one's place among the Best. Apart from all the silly little ones about language and dress, there were three which went deeper: one was supposed not to be a coward, not to tell lies, and above all not to be vain and boastful. I say 'above all' because that was the rule against which infantile rumbustiousness most often stubbed a toe: YOU ARE NOT THE ONLY PEBBLE ON THE BEACH might have been inscribed above the nursery door, and I know several people, some of them dear to me, who still feel its truth so acutely that only with difficulty (if at all) can they forgive a book written in the first person about that person's life.

I soon came to see our tribal complacency as ridiculous, and can claim that I never slipped back into it, but the mood it engendered is another matter: it was based on nonsense – on wicked non-sense – but it was sustaining, it made one feel sure of oneself. I was robbed of that mood (by being rejected, more than by seeing through class smugness and imperialism, though that must have modified it a good deal), and such a deprivation – the smashing of self-confidence – whatever its cause, makes a person feel horribly chilly. Now, however, having become pleased with myself in other ways, I recognize the return of the comfortable warmth I knew in early youth. If this is smugness, and I can't help feeling that it is, then I have to report that I have learnt through experience that, though repulsive to witness, it is a far more comfortable state *to be in* than its opposite. And comfort one does need, because there's no denying that moving through advanced old age is a downhill jour-ney. You start with what is good about it, or at least less disagreeable than you expected, and if you have been, or are being, exceptionally lucky you naturally make the most of that, but 'at my back I always hear / Time's wingèd chariot hurrying near', and that is sobering, to say the least of it. For one thing, it's a constant reminder of matters much larger than oneself.

There is, for example, the thought quite common among us who are old: 'Well, thank god I shan't be here to see *that*.' Try as you may not to brood about global warming, *there it is*, and it doesn't go away because I shan't see much of it, or because, having no children, I don't have to worry about their experience of it . . . All that happens when I try to use that for comfort is the looming up of other people's children. I suppose there is a slight relief in the knowledge that you, personally, will not have to bear it, but it is unaccompanied by the pleasure usually expected from relief.

And that capaciousness of life, the variety within it which at first seems so impressive – what does that do after a while but remind you of its opposite, the tininess of a life even when seen against the scale of nothing bigger than human existence? Thought of in that light the unimportance of the individual is dizzying, so what have I been doing, thinking and tapping away at 'I this' and 'I that'? I too, as well as my dear disapprovers, ask that question – though with a built-in expectation, I must admit, of justification.

Because after all, minuscule though every individual, every 'self', is, he/she/it is an object through which life is being expressed, and leaves some sort of contribution to the world. The majority of human beings leave their genes embodied in other human beings, others things they have made, everyone things they have done: they have taught or tortured, built or bombed, dug a garden or chopped down trees, so that our whole environment, cities, farmland, deserts – the lot! – is built up of contributions, useful or detrimental, from the innumerable swarm of selfs preceding us, to which we ourselves are adding our grains of sand. To think our existence pointless, as atheists are supposed by some religious people to do, would therefore be absurd; instead, we should remember that it does make its almost invisible but real contribution, either to usefulness or harm, which is why we should try to conduct it properly. So an individual life *is* interesting enough to merit examination, and my own is the only one I really know (as Jean Rhys, faced with this same worry, always used to say), and if it is to be examined, it should be examined as honestly as is possible within the examiner's inevitable limitations. To do it otherwise is pointless – and also makes very boring reading, as witness many autobiographies by celebrities of one sort or another.

What dies is not a life's value, but the worn-out (or damaged) container of the self, together with the self's awareness of itself: away that goes into nothingness, with everyone else's. That is what is so disconcerting to an onlooker, because unless someone slips away while unconscious, a person who is just about to die is still fully alive and fully her or himself – I remember thinking as I sat beside my mother 'But she *can't* be dying, because she's still so entirely here' (the wonderful words which turned out to be her last, 'It was absolutely divine', were not intended as such but were just part of something she was telling me). The difference between being and non-being is both so abrupt and so vast that it remains shocking even though it happens to every living thing that is, was, or ever will be. (What Henry James was thinking of when he called death 'distinguished', when it is the commonest thing in life, I can't imagine – though the poor old man was at his last gasp when he said it, so one ought not to carp.)

No doubt one likes the idea of 'last words' because they soften the shock. Given the physical nature of the act of dying, one has to suppose that most of the pithy ones are apocryphal, but still one likes to imagine oneself signing off in a memorable way, and a reason why I have sometimes been sorry that I don't believe in God is that I shan't, in fairness, be able to quote 'Dieu me pardonnerai, c'est son metier', words which have always made me laugh and which, besides, are wonderfully sensible. As it is, what I would like to say is: 'It's all right. Don't mind not knowing.' And foolish though it may be, I have to confess that I still hope the occasion on which I have to say it does not come very soon.